OCCASIONAL P

Albania: From Isolation Toward Reform

Mario I. Blejer, Mauro Mecagni, Ratna Sahay,
Richard Hides, Barry Johnston, Piroska Nagy, and Roy Pepper

INTERNATIONAL MONETARY FUND
Washington DC
September 1992

© 1992 International Monetary Fund

Library of Congress Cataloging-in-Publication Data

Albania, from isolation toward reform / Mario I. Blejer ... [et al.].
    p. cm. — (Occasional paper / International Monetary Fund,
ISSN 0251-6365 ; 98)
   Includes bibliographical references (p.).
   ISBN 1-55775-266-4
   1. Albania—Economic conditions. 2. Albania—Economic
policy.
I. Bléjer, Mario I. II. Series: Occasional paper (International
Monetary Fund) ; no. 98.
HC402.A63   1992
330.94965—dc20   92-24707
                                                  CIP

Price: US$15.00
(US$12.00 to full-time faculty members and
students at universities and colleges)

Please send orders to:
International Monetary Fund, Publication Services
700 19th Street, N.W., Washington, D.C. 20431, U.S.A.
Telephone: (202) 623-7430   Telefax: (202) 623-7201

Contents

	Page

Tables

Page

Appendix

Charts

Section

The following symbols have been used throughout this paper:

. . .   to indicate that data are not available;

—   to indicate that the figure is zero or less than half the final digit shown, or that the item does not exist;

–   between years or months (e.g., 1991–92 or January–June) to indicate the years or months covered, including the beginning and ending years or months;

/   between years (e.g., 1991/92) to indicate a crop or fiscal (financial) year.

"Billion" means a thousand million.

Minor discrepancies between constituent figures and totals are due to rounding.

The term "country," as used in this paper, does not in all cases refer to a territorial entity that is a state as understood by international law and practice; the term also covers some territorial entities that are not states, but for which statistical data are maintained and provided internationally on a separate and independent basis.

Preface

This paper is based on a report prepared by Mario Blejer (World Bank), Mauro Mecagni, Ratna Sahay (all Eastern European Division, European I Department), Richard Hides (Statistics Department), Barry Johnston (Policy Development and Review Department), Piroska Nagy (Central Division, European II Department), and Roy Pepper (World Bank) in connection with the application of Albania for membership in the IMF. Any opinions expressed are those of the authors and should not be construed as reflecting the views of the Albanian authorities, Executive Directors of the IMF, or other IMF staff members. The authors bear the sole responsibility for any errors.

The authors gratefully acknowledge the assistance enthusiastically extended by the many Albanian officials with whom they worked during several visits to Tirana. They are grateful to Samir Fawzi, Kenneth Friedman, Joshua Greene, Aarno Liuksila, Orlando Roncesvalles, and Mohammad Shadman-Valavi who, as part of the Albanian team, also contributed to this study. Thanks are also due to Manuel Guitián and Anoop Singh for their comments, to Anne Williams, Divina Tenorio, and Nahid Mejid for secretarial support, and to Barbara Kaminska for research assistance. The paper was edited by Elin Knotter of the External Relations Department.

1 Introduction

An Overview

Until the beginning of 1991, and for more than four decades, Albania was one of the least known and less accessible countries in the world. It secluded itself in self-imposed isolation and was ruled by an authoritarian regime that professed to adhere strictly to Marxist ideology and Stalinist practices in an attempt to carry out one of the most far-reaching experiments in socialist orthodoxy. Although not much was known about the country's economy, Albania was usually characterized as the poorest and least developed nation in Europe, probably the only one in the continent with standards of living resembling Third World countries.

Although initially regarded as a bastion of resistance against the radical changes taking place in the socialist world, Albania had, by the middle of 1991, joined the reform movement sweeping through Eastern Europe. In June 1991, the first noncommunist multiparty coalition government in the postwar era was formed. Diplomatic relations with many countries were renewed, and Albania joined the International Monetary Fund (October 15, 1991), the World Bank, and the European Bank for Reconstruction and Development, among other international organizations.

As Albania attempts to reform its system and rejoin the world economic community, and as more information about the country becomes available, the picture that emerges is one of an economy in the midst of a very serious and profound crisis that is probably deeper than that experienced by other reforming socialist countries. It is undergoing a drastic contraction in economic activity (30–40 percent during 1990–91), a sharp deterioration in its external accounts, a virtual exhaustion of foreign exchange reserves, and a rapid buildup of external debt and arrears.

In this context, the newly available information on the evolution of key economic and financial variables in recent years, as well as on the intricacies of the policies followed, assists in the search for the roots of the current crisis. Although it could be claimed that such fundamental reforms as the abandonment of central planning and the embracing of a market-oriented system would relegate the study of even the most recent economic developments in reforming countries to the realm of economic history, it is clear that the understanding of events and of the framework within which they have taken place could contribute considerably to the design of appropriate solutions. This paper seeks to present a complete and concise picture of the traditional Albanian economic system, much of which still exists, an analysis of the main economic developments and policies during the 1980s, and an account of the most recent evolution of the economy, as well as of the unfolding of the economic reform process.

The present economic crisis in Albania is not just the consequence of recent events. It reflects the buildup of structural problems, policy mismanagement, and financial imbalances deeply rooted in the development strategy followed since World War II. Like other socialist economies, Albania's economic model was based on two principles: complete reliance on central planning and rejection of private ownership of means of production. Although enforcement of these principles was carried to an extreme unknown in many other socialist countries, and almost *all* forms of private property were eliminated, the "Albanian model" was unique in that it included a third principle: the idealization of national self-reliance as a guiding tenet of economic policy, which, in practical terms, gave a central role to the pursuit of economic autarky. This strategy was symbolized by the constitutional ban on external credit, aid, and investment that was adopted in 1976 and culminated in the self-imposed financial isolation of Albania in the 1980s.

Until about the end of the 1970s, the Albanian economy followed the path of some other small developing countries—socialist and nonsocialist alike—in disregarding economic incentives, the central role of market forces, the principle of comparative advantage, and the importance of financial discipline. As a result, economic performance was impaired by relative price distortions, by the

Box I. A Profile of Albania

Albania is located in the Balkan peninsula in southeastern Europe, on the eastern shore of the Strait of Otranto across from Italy. It is bordered by Yugoslavia to the north and east, by Greece to the south, and by the Adriatic and Ionian Seas to the west.

The smallest of the Balkan countries, it has an area of 11,100 square miles (28,748 square kilometers), a population of 3.26 million, and GDP per capita estimated at slightly more than $600 in 1990. Albania is predominantly mountainous—roughly three fourths of its territory consists of mountains and hills in the northern, central, and southern parts at elevations over 200 meters above sea level. In contrast to the rugged terrain and limited arable land in the mountainous regions, the western plains beside the Adriatic Sea are endowed with very fertile soil.

Reflecting a varied geological structure, Albania has a wealth of natural resources, including chromium, copper, iron/nickel, coal/lignite, oil, bauxite, phosphorate, asbestos, bituminous sands, pyrites and nickel silicate, as well as limestone, sands, marble, and clays. The major resources currently exploited are chromium (third largest producer in the world), copper, iron/nickel, limestone, phosphorate, and coal.

Compared with other European countries, the agricultural sector (including forestry) is relatively important; during the 1980s, it accounted for 33 percent of the country's net material product (NMP), and employed nearly 50 percent of the total working population. The share of the industrial sector in NMP was 44 percent, while that in employment was 22 percent. The remainder was accounted for by the services sector, of which construction activity was the most significant. Transportation and communications systems are poorly developed and are similar to those in low-income developing countries.

Table I. Social Indicators[1]

GDP per capita (*current U.S. dollars, 1990*)	623[2]
Population and vital statistics (*1990*)	
Total population (*in thousands*)	3,256
Population growth rate (*in percent*)	1.8
Life expectancy at birth (*in years*)	
Male	69.6
Female	75.5
Population age structure (*in percent*)	
Under working age (0–14)	32.8
Working age (15–59 for men, 15–54 for women)	57.8
Over working age (60 and above for men, 55 and above for women)	9.4
Crude birth rate (*per thousand*)	24.7
Crude death rate (*per thousand*)	5.7
Infant mortality rate (*per thousand*)	39.0
Food, health, and nutrition	
Per capita supply of	
Calories (*per day*)	2,713
Proteins (*grams per day*)	82
Labor force (*1990*)	
Total labor force (*in thousands*)	1,567
Female (*in percent*)	48.1
Agriculture[3] (*in percent*)	49.1
Industry (*in percent*)	22.7
Education	
Enrollment rates (*percent of school-age children*)	
Primary	96.0
Secondary	70.0
Colleges, specialized schools, and universities	25.7
Pupil/teacher ratio	
Primary	19.4
Secondary	21.7
Other	
Private cars (*per thousand*)	—[4]
Radios (*percentage of families*)	73.8
Televisions (*percentage of families*)	48.0
Washing machines (*percentage of families*)	12.7
Refrigerators (*percentage of families*)	14.1

Sources: Data provided by the Albanian authorities; and World Bank, *Social Indicators of Development*, 1989.
[1] Refers to most recent year (usually 1989) for which data are available.
[2] At commercial exchange rate of leks 8 = $1.
[3] Includes forestry.
[4] Permitted only since the second half of 1990.

financial burden of consumer and enterprise subsidies associated with a system of rigidly fixed prices, and by a pattern of production specialization that led to mounting mismatches between supply and demand. For a time, however, the consequences of these policies were concealed by Albania's access to substantial external resources, from the then U.S.S.R. in the 1950s and from China in the 1960s and 1970s. This transfer of external savings not only allowed the system to neglect the cumulative effects of policy mistakes but also fueled slow but steady growth and even enabled the accumulation of significant foreign exchange reserves.

Albania's distinctive experience began, however, in 1978 when it interrupted economic and financial relations with China and felt the full enforcement of the 1976 constitutional ban on all forms of foreign finance. Although many countries have been able to cope with the cessation of foreign financing, it usually requires macroeconomic adjustments. Albania did not adjust to the new situation, and aggregate demand, fueled by monetary growth and fiscal imbalances, continued to grow rapidly. Moreover, to manage the economy in conditions of financial autarky, it was necessary to tighten state command of the system further, thereby aggravating the misallocation of resources. This also accelerated the decline in productivity caused by the Government's commitment to provide employment for a rapidly increasing labor force and by the continuous deterioration and technological obsolescence of the capital stock, which had been outdated already at installation. Under such circumstances economic growth decelerated substantially, from nearly 5 percent in the 1970s to an annual average of about 1 percent during the 1980s.

Nevertheless, the crisis was able to be postponed for almost a decade because of the past accumulation of foreign exchange reserves, the ability to maintain a broadly balanced current account in nonconvertible currencies, favorable developments in Albania's terms of trade, and new exports of primary commodities. But over time the accumulated repercussions from the intensified macroeconomic imbalances, along with growing fiscal deficits and rapid monetary expansion (especially in the second half of the 1980s) and increasing shortages of consumer goods, became fully apparent. Moreover, most recently, the consequences of protracted microeconomic distortions and macroeconomic mismanagement were exposed further through the increased import requirements arising from domestic supply bottlenecks, the collapse of export markets in Eastern Europe, the adverse turnaround in the terms of trade, and the depletion of foreign reserves.

In 1990, the fiscal situation deteriorated markedly, with the deficit reaching a level of over 16 percent of GDP. Monetary expansion exceeded 20 percent, reforms were undertaken only timidly, and, in a striking reversal of the previous policy of abstinence from foreign financial sources, substantial payments arrears with foreign commercial banks rapidly accumulated, severely damaging Albania's reputation in international financial markets. Although exceptionally adverse weather in 1990 contributed to the sharp decline in output, the continued collapse in production carried over into 1991, with a severe aggravation of financial imbalances. Under such conditions, the road to recovery requires not only decisive macroeconomic adjustment but also a complete overhaul of the economic system through the adoption of a comprehensive program of institutional and structural transformation. The initial steps toward that goal through the end of 1991 are described in Section V of this paper.

Historical and Political Background

Albanians are believed to be descendants of the Illyrians, an Indo-European tribe, who began inhabiting the Balkan peninsula about four thousand years ago. The term, Albania, is derived from the name of an Illyrian tribe, Albanoi, who are believed to have inhabited the central part of present-day Albania. The Romans conquered the Illyrian territories and ruled for more than five centuries. After the decline of the Roman Empire, the Illyrian territories continued to be subjected to foreign invasion—the Goths and the Huns in the fourth century, the Bulgars in the fifth century, the Slavs in the sixth and seventh centuries, the Normans in the eleventh and twelfth centuries, and the Serbs in the fourteenth century.

At the end of the fourteenth century the Ottomans invaded Albania. Skanderbeg, the most revered Albanian hero, successfully fended them off for twenty-five years. After his death in 1468, Albania became a part of the Ottoman Empire, and a predominantly Christian population was brought under the influence of Islam during this period. (In 1967 Albania became the first self-proclaimed atheist country and strictly outlawed all religious practices. At that time, Albanians were roughly 70 percent Muslim and the rest Christian, mostly of Eastern Orthodox denomination.) Albanian nationalist movements began to gain prominence during the second half of the

Table 2. Main Economic Indicators

	Average 1980–85	1986	1987	1988	1989	1990	Preliminary 1991
	(Percentage change)						
Net material product	1.6	6.2	−2.2	−0.5	11.7	−13.1	...
Personal consumption	2.5	4.6	3.4	1.1	6.9	2.0	...
(in percent of GDP)	50.9	51.9	54.1	55.5	54.0	63.4	...
Social consumption	2.2	0.4	3.1	−1.7	2.2	0.4	...
(in percent of GDP)	8.7	8.5	8.8	8.8	8.2	9.4	...
Net capital formation	−0.8	3.6	−17.0	13.3	30.6	−30.5	...
(in percent of GDP)	20.2	17.6	14.7	16.9	20.1	16.1	...
Gross domestic product	2.0	5.6	−0.8	−1.4	9.8	−13.1	−30
	(In millions of leks)						
Net material product	13,392	14,013	13,700	13,631	15,223	13,229	...
Gross domestic product	16,376	17,390	17,254	17,008	18,681	16,234	...
	(Percentage change)						
Gross industrial production	2.6	5.0	1.5	2.1	5.0	−7.5	−37
Gross agricultural production	3.0	4.0	0.5	−6.2	10.7	−7.4	−24
Population growth	2.1	2.0	2.0	2.0	1.9	1.8	2.0
Employment growth	3.0	3.3	3.0	1.7	1.9	0.2	...
Total unemployment rate	4.3	5.4	5.2	6.0	6.7	8.5	...
Retail prices (period average)	−0.3	—	—	—	—	—	36
Wholesale industrial prices	−0.6	—	—	—	—	—	...
Average effective earnings[1]	1.2	1.1	−1.8	0.5	4.7	−1.5	...
	(In millions of leks)						
State budget revenues	8,475.8[2]	8,473	8,488	9,052	9,003	7,630	5,200
(in percent of GDP)	50.9[2]	48.7	49.2	53.2	48.2	47.0	32
State budget expenditure[3]	8,908.7[2]	8,481.7	8,776.1	9,255.9	10,603.7	10,331.5	10,200
(in percent of GDP)	53.5[2]	48.8	50.9	54.4	56.8	63.6	64
Fiscal balance[3,4]	−432.9[2]	−8.7	−288.1	−203.9	−1,600.7	−2,701.5	−5,500
(in percent of GDP)	−2.6[2]	−0.1	−1.7	−1.2	−8.6	−16.6	−34
	(Percentage change)						
Total domestic credit	7.5	3.5	12.8	−0.7	21.5	21.9	80
Broad money	3.5	7.3	7.2	7.8	14.8	21.0	110
(in percent of GDP)	17.6	19.6	21.1	23.1	24.1	33.7	67
Currency in circulation	6.6	7.0	12.3	6.2	0.6	36.5	169
	(Convertible currencies, in millions of U.S. dollars)						
Current account balance	−27.6	0.5	7.8	−23.5	−70.4	−95.1	−250
Trade balance	−33.2	−0.6	1.0	−34.8	−90.9	−109.6	−209
Exports	116.6	95.5	100.3	106.6	132.7	123.0	72
Imports	149.8	96.1	99.3	141.4	223.6	232.6	281
Net international reserves[5]	171.1	110.1	119.8	80.4	−63.0	−317.2	−527
	(Nonconvertible currencies, in millions of rubles)						
Current account balance	2.0	−4.5	−0.6	−13.5	18.8	−44.9	−7
Trade balance	−0.2	−9.0	−6.3	−18.6	15.0	−48.6	−5
	(Nonconvertible currencies other than ruble, in millions of U.S. dollars)						
Current account balance	6.6	0.8	−1.9	−16.1	−2.5	−14.4	−25
Trade balance	9.1	4.3	0.9	−10.3	−1.2	−11.6	−26
Commercial exchange rate *(leks/dollar)*	8.7	8.0	8.0	8.0	8.0	8.0	10–25
Commercial exchange rate *(leks/ruble)*	11.4	8.0	8.0	8.0	8.0	8.0	...

Source: Data provided by the Albanian authorities.
[1] Includes bonuses.
[2] 1982–85.
[3] On a commitment basis.
[4] Excluding grants.
[5] Including assets in nonconvertible currencies and gold valued at market prices.

nineteenth century, but it was not until 1912 that Ismail Quemal proclaimed the country's independence. After a period of political turmoil during World War I (1914–18) and for some time thereafter, King Zog ruled during 1928–39, exercising absolute power.

During World War II (1939–45), the country was annexed by Italy (1939) and later occupied by Germany (1943). The Allied forces never occupied Albania; it was freed from German occupation by local partisans affiliated with the Albanian Communist Party (founded in 1941), militarily supported by the Anglo-American command in Italy, and politically backed by the Yugoslav Communist Party. In effect, the Albanian communists, with a strong political organization and substantial armed partisan groups, filled a political vacuum that existed after the war.

After November 1944 Albania experienced an uninterrupted period of strong centralist rule under Enver Hoxha, the unchallenged communist leader until his death in 1985. Centralism, in the Albanian context, meant both centralized planning and direction of the economy and central control of the political, social, and cultural life of the country and its people.

Albania's turbulent and long historical experience with repeated foreign invasion had instilled a strong sense of patriotic fervor and nationalism in its people and set the background for the fiercely independent foreign policy of the new government, reflected in dramatic shifts in Albania's foreign alliances. After World War II, the political position of the Albanian Government was initially influenced by the Yugoslavs (1945–48), followed by the Soviets (1949–61) and the Chinese (1961–78). Albania joined the Council for Mutual Economic Assistance (CMEA) in 1949 but withdrew in 1961.

The break with Yugoslavia in 1948 was an outcome of the Albanians' concern that Yugoslavia had plans to incorporate Albania as its seventh republic. The alliance with the former Soviet Union was financially rewarding, but Albania was deeply committed to the Stalinist model of heavy-industry-led development and felt compelled to shun Soviet pressure to develop its raw material base. Following ideological and political tensions, the diplomatic and financial ties with the former U.S.S.R. were broken in 1961, and China became Albania's closest ally. However, after Mao's death in 1976, the Chinese-Albanian relationship suffered a political setback and by 1978 the break with China was complete. In 1976 a new Constitution was adopted (see Box 2 for details), which abolished all remaining private property and banned foreign aid, credit, and investment.

After Hoxha's death in 1985, Ramiz Alia became leader of the Communist Party and President of Albania. Since 1986, Albania has begun to show an interest in emerging from its isolation and in improving relations with the West. The dramatic collapse of the communist regimes in Bulgaria, Czechoslovakia, the former German Democratic Republic, Hungary, Poland, and Romania set the stage for the fall of the last bastion of Stalinist rule in Eastern Europe. However, it was not until the second half of 1990 that a democratization process began with the formation of opposition parties, and the first pluralistic elections were held in March 1991. The Albanian Labor Party emerged with an absolute majority, but the Government collapsed under pressure of increasing unrest and dissatisfaction among the population. In June 1991, a coalition government was formed. New elections were held in March 1992, with the Democratic Party winning a clear majority.

II The Pre-Reform Economic System

A complete chronological description of the evolution of the Albanian economic system is precluded by the very tight controls on information that existed over a long period. Consequently, few, if any, documents are available to help in constructing a comprehensive and accurate picture of Albania's modern economic history.

It is known that at the end of World War II Albania was predominantly an agricultural society with practically no industrial base, and that its substantial natural resources were largely untapped. Following the advent of the communist regime in November 1944, Albania's economic performance and its economic system were influenced mostly by political and ideological factors. From that time, the economic system evolved strictly along the lines of the classic Stalinist model: central planning dominated all economic activity, decision making was strongly hierarchical, and the achievement of physical production targets became the primary goal of economic policy. This model, with few changes, prevailed until mid-1990.

Evolution of Stalinist System

State Ownership

A distinctive feature of the Albanian economy was that virtually all productive units became, over time, either state or collectively owned and private property virtually disappeared. The first economic step of the socialist government was to nationalize all public utilities and foreign capital in 1946. Local businessmen were taxed at prohibitive levels, resulting in the expropriation of their property. By early 1947, the state had taken over domestic industry and foreign trade.

In the agricultural sector, in accordance with the agrarian laws of 1945–46, the communist government confiscated all large estates and redistributed them among farmers, limiting the maximum size for each family holding to five hectares. Contrary to developments in the industrial sector, collectiv-

ization of agriculture was slow: it started in 1946, gained momentum after 1955, and was completed only in 1967. This pace was largely the result of the rugged Albanian terrain, which is not suitable for collectivization. The Constitution—adopted in 1976—legalized the nationalization of all land, including agricultural land. A holdover from private activity remained—cultivation by cooperative members for their own consumption on small plots and the raising of livestock on these plots. In 1981, however, livestock-rearing was also subjected to forced collectivization, which, in turn, led to mass slaughtering and drastically reduced the meat supply in the ensuing years.

Internal trading activity was fully state owned and controlled until mid-1990, and external trade until April 1991. External trade was carried out by a few state enterprises specializing in foreign trade. Domestically, consumer goods were distributed through shops and store outlets of the internal trading state enterprises and also, to a limited extent, by cooperatives. The provision of social services, such as education and health services, was also fully vested in the state. In addition, practically all houses in urban areas and those occupied by state farm workers were constructed and owned by the state. In contrast, houses in the cooperative sector were owner financed and belonged to cooperative workers.

Central Planning

By 1951, practically all forms of market mechanism in Albania had been replaced by central planning. All economic decisions on production, pricing, wage setting, investment, and external trade were centralized and implemented within the context of five-year plans. Prices and wages were fixed and remained largely unchanged throughout each planning period, and changes between the plans were generally minimal. The domestic price of traded goods was largely insulated from external influences by a system of taxes and subsidies.

A four-tier decision-making hierarchy was instituted. At the highest level was the Council of

Box 2. Strengthening of State Control: New Constitution of 1976

To replace the Constitution introduced in 1946 and revised in 1950, Albania adopted a new Constitution in 1976. The "new economic order" set out in this Constitution effectively isolated the country from the rest of the world and extended the state's control over virtually all aspects of the lives of its people.

The new Constitution was unique in many respects. Drafted by a commission headed by Enver Hoxha, it sanctioned the one-party system in accordance with Marxist-Leninist doctrine. The Albanian Party of Labor (APL) and the state became completely intertwined; for example, the First Secretary of the Party's Central Committee was designated commander-in-chief of the armed forces, thereby controlling any potential threat to the APL. Albania was the only communist country that had officially abrogated institutionalized religion in 1967; the Constitution of 1976 legalized this decision.

A ban on credit and investment from abroad, unparalleled in any other country, was introduced. The concept of a "socialist economy" based on the socialist ownership of all means of production was introduced by abolishing all but minimal categories of personal property.

Although the Constitution guaranteed the citizens certain inalienable rights, such as equal treatment under the law, work, rest, and health, as well as freedom of speech, press, organization, assembly, and public demonstration, opinion contrary to the APL's ideology was totally suppressed. Because a very small percentage of the population (less than 4 percent in 1990) were members of the APL, the party depended considerably on mass organizations, primarily those of youth, women, and labor unions, to achieve its goals in the political, social, and economic spheres.

Ministers, followed by the branch ministries, executive committees (equivalent to the local government), and state enterprises. Branch ministries functioned at the national level, and executive committees at the district level. Executive committees were in charge of all the enterprises in each of the 26 districts and generally reported to the appropriate branch ministries. Since information flowed strictly vertically, the intermediate levels were in frequent negotiation with the Council of Ministers and the state enterprises.

The State Planning Commission (SPC), directly subordinate to the Council of Ministers, was in charge of formulating a detailed plan prescribing the physical quantities to be met by each productive unit. The SPC drew up the country's first national plan, the nine-month plan of April–December 1947. This plan was relatively simple, with no global indicators for the economy. Subsequent plans during 1948–50[1] became progressively more complex, with macroeconomic targets for growth and investment and detailed planning of physical output, material balances, and input utilization norms for enterprises.

The country's First Five-Year Plan was prepared with Soviet assistance and launched in 1951. There was a clear bias in favor of industry, particularly heavy industry and the mineral sector. By 1959, the complete Soviet system of plan indica-

tors was adopted, including lists of projects, global output, output mix, input requirements, use of productive capacity, volume and structure of capital investment, labor productivity and employment, training of new workers, wage fund, average wages, unit production costs, and sales. Few changes were introduced until very recently.

Goods shortages frequently emerged, and rationing was used to allocate goods among consumers. Before 1957, the Government operated a dual-pricing system for consumer goods whereby a ration or a "ticket" amount could be obtained at low prices, and further supplies were frequently available at higher, although still administratively set, prices. In 1957, on Soviet advice, the Government unified agricultural prices and raised them to levels between those prevailing in the two markets. These prices have remained largely unchanged, setting the base for increasing subsidies from the budget. A one-time wage adjustment was also given in 1957 to offset the impact of the price increases, and no significant price and wage policy changes have occurred since.

As in other centrally planned economies, labor mobility has been low. Each enterprise had a well-defined employment structure and was allocated a fixed number of workers, paid from a centrally determined wage fund. Since full employment was an explicit government goal, it was not uncommon for the Government to increase the number of workers in an enterprise without a corresponding increase in labor demand by the enterprise. Workers were frequently expected to work overtime on a "voluntary" basis to compensate for their low productivity.

---

[1]A one-year plan was adopted in 1948, followed by a two-year plan in 1949–50. The main objective of the two-year plan was to repair war damage and restore the economy to its prewar level.

Financial Policies

The state budget was tightly linked to the financial position of the state enterprises. Before the mid-1990 reforms, more than 90 percent of the profits and close to 70 percent of the amortization funds of state enterprises were administratively transferred to the budget. In turn, the budget was responsible for financing all state enterprises' investments and for covering all their losses. Because domestic prices of traded goods were fixed domestically, the losses and profits from foreign transactions were also reflected in the budget.

Money and credit played a passive role. There was no monetary policy as such, with the central bank (the State Bank of Albania) merely transferring resources for meeting the plan targets. All transfers between the budget and the state enterprises, as well as between the enterprises, were routed through the bank. In effect, the bank provided a check on the activities of state enterprises to ensure that the plans were being appropriately implemented.

Until August 1990, foreign transactions were fully centralized. An annual foreign exchange budget or plan approved by the Government set out the planned total value of exports and imports in the domestic currency (leks), as well as the enterprise targets for exports and their quotas for imports in convertible and nonconvertible currencies. No customs duties or tariffs were applied to exports and imports under the foreign exchange plan. The State Bank of Albania had a foreign exchange monopoly until 1990, as all foreign exchange transactions had to be routed through, and foreign exchange surrendered to, the bank.

After the Second World War, the official value of the lek was established on the basis of its gold content. Official exchange rates (quoted against the dollar and the ruble) were announced and used for accounting and statistical purposes up to 1985, and commercial exchange rates were announced and used for these purposes thereafter. Although before 1986 commercial exchange rates were also calculated (but not announced), they were known as "economic exchange rates." Since domestic prices were set independently of international prices,[2] these economic exchange rates were used to convert prices of traded goods quoted in foreign currency to their lek equivalents. They were calculated for the dollar and ruble by relating the value of the exports in leks (wholesale prices times quantity of exports) to the export value received in

foreign currency. Different exchange rates were also applied to a limited list of noncommercial transactions.

Economic Organization of Enterprises

Two principal forms of productive units existed in the economy: state enterprises operating in the agricultural, industrial, and trading sectors, and agricultural cooperatives.

The state enterprises were typically horizontally and vertically integrated and were therefore very large. Average employment levels were more than 700 workers per enterprise in 1989, with the largest enterprises employing more than 4,000 workers. Until 1947, state enterprises operated as budgetary institutions; their expenses were covered by the state budget, and all their output was surrendered to the Government. Beginning in 1948, the Government moved the state enterprises out of the budget and made them into "self-accounting enterprises," but without autonomy and fully subject to central planning.

Like other government institutions, the internal organization of the state enterprises has been hierarchical. The enterprise directors had no economic decision-making power and relied completely on directives from the relevant branch ministry or the executive committee. While investment decisions were made by the state and channeled through the state budget, all other inputs were supplied in accordance with the central plan of the branch ministry or the executive committee.

As a result of growing dissatisfaction among workers in the mid-1960s, Hoxha launched a "Cultural and Ideological Revolution" whose objective was to strengthen control by the Albanian Party of Labor (APL) over all aspects of society. To placate dissatisfied enterprise workers, an attempt was made in 1965 to increase incentives by streamlining the planning process. Henceforth, instead of receiving a detailed plan from the state hierarchy, workers were induced to discuss broad plan targets, which would then be sent to the higher authorities for approval. The ultimate decision-making power, however, remained with the central planners.

Some attempts at decentralization of decision-making were also introduced in the state hierarchy; primary responsibility in many areas shifted from the Council of Ministers to the branch ministries and the executive committees. In 1960, only 20 percent of the enterprises were under the jurisdiction of the executive committees; this number had increased to 40 percent in 1969 and to 80 percent in 1971. Unlike other Central and East European countries, however, the position of Al-

---

[2]An exception was made in setting domestic wholesale prices of imported capital goods (Section III).

banian managers continually deteriorated. During the late 1960s and the 1970s, the typical manager faced several salary cutbacks. With the introduction of workers' participation, the managers' authority over the activities of the state enterprises diminished. Not only were they under pressure from the state hierarchy and the workers' organization to set high targets, but they were also held responsible for underachievement and poor performance. Moreover, conflict between managers and workers on questions of underachievement was strongly discouraged. Poor performance by workers was always explained—not by the lack of economic incentives—but by inadequate ideological indoctrination of the workers. Although these changes seem to have been successful in ensuring popular support for the APL, they had little impact on the system of incentives or on economic decision making, which continued to be concentrated in the state hierarchy.

Before 1985 there were no penalties for enterprise losses, but thereafter a system of points was established based on realized production, proportion of contracts met, costs incurred, and workers' productivity. If the enterprise recorded a number of points below a critical level, salaries could be cut up to 10 percent annually. There were, of course, no provisions for bankruptcy during this period.

Agricultural cooperatives differed from agricultural state enterprises mainly in terms of their financial relationship with the budget (less than 10 percent of their profits were transferred to the budget while most of their investments were financed either by bank loans or were self financed) and in terms of their wage policy (internally determined and a function of the revenues they generated). Although plan targets set for the cooperatives were meant to be indicative, the cooperatives were usually compelled to implement them.

III Economic Performance in the 1980s

By the beginning of World War II, more than 85 percent of the Albanian population derived its livelihood from a poorly developed agricultural sector, which contributed roughly the same proportion to output. The vast mineral resources of the country (such as oil, copper, chromium, and ferro-nickel) were largely untapped. There were only small-scale and handicraft industries, most employing no more than 15 workers. The Communist Government made rapid industrialization one of its principal aims. Between 1951 and 1975, the Albanian economy experienced high growth rates and striking structural transformation (Chart 1).[3] The growth of NMP from one five-year plan to the next was, on average, nearly 44 percent, with industry recording the fastest rates during this period (Table 3). The share of agriculture declined from 80 percent during the First Five-Year Plan (1951–55) to 36 percent in the Fifth Five-Year Plan (1971–75), while the corresponding figures for industry were 14 percent and 35 percent, respectively. Within industry, the mineral sector and electricity generation were primarily developed, and financial and technical assistance from the former U.S.S.R. and China during this period was highly instrumental in establishing a large industrial base by the end of the 1970s. At the same time the economy faced large balance of payments

---

[3]As in other East European countries, national accounts in Albania are based on the system of material product balances (MPS), which divides economic activity into material and nonmaterial spheres. The material sphere, which contributes to the net material product (NMP), comprises those branches of production that directly create material goods, such as industry, agriculture, and construction. In addition, transportation, telecommunications, and retail trade are included, as they are considered to add to the value of material goods. The nonmaterial sphere is broadly composed of education, sports, cultural activities, research, public health, national defense, financial services, social services, and services of voluntary organizations.

Economic trends in this section are discussed primarily on the basis of the NMP concept. GDP estimates have also been derived using the methodology of the UN System of National Accounts (SNA) (Appendix Table 1).

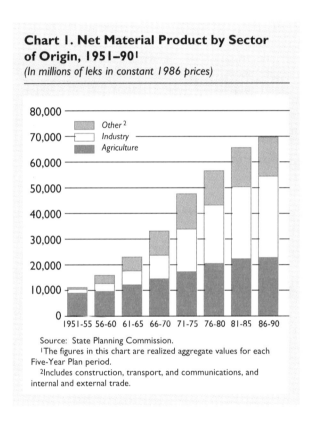

Chart 1. Net Material Product by Sector of Origin, 1951–90[1]
(In millions of leks in constant 1986 prices)

Source: State Planning Commission.
[1]The figures in this chart are realized aggregate values for each Five-Year Plan period.
[2]Includes construction, transport, and communications, and internal and external trade.

deficits that were financed by Soviet and Chinese capital inflows.

Output Growth and Composition

In contrast with the previous period, the 1980s witnessed a strong slowdown in economic activity, which virtually stagnated during the second half of the decade, reflecting Albania's self-imposed isolation since 1978 and the emergence of serious internal and external imbalances. While real NMP had grown by nearly 44 percent between the Fourth (1966–70) and the Fifth Plans (1971–75), and by about 20 percent between the Fifth and the Sixth Plans (1976–80) (Table 3), it rose by an average of less than 1 percent a year between 1980–89, declining from an average of 1.6 percent

Table 3. Net Material Product by Sector of Origin, 1951–90[1]
(In millions of leks, in constant 1986 prices)

	1951–55	1956–60	1961–65	1966–70	1971–75	1976–80	1981–85	1986–90
Net material product	11,223	16,003	23,078	33,170	47,704	56,672	65,725	69,796
Agriculture	9,025	9,643	12,215	14,586	17,325	20,533	22,315	22,822
Industry	1,520	3,099	5,531	9,191	16,577	22,793	28,092	31,691
Construction	. . .	1,073	1,761	2,421	3,374	3,915	4,948	4,554
Transport and communications	. . .	295	559	727	1,390	1,662	2,156	2,423
Other	. . .	1,893	3,012	6,245	9,038	7,769	8,214	8,305
(Aggregate percentage change over previous plan period)								
Net material product	. . .	42.6	44.2	43.7	43.8	18.8	16.0	6.2
Agriculture	. . .	6.8	26.7	19.4	18.8	18.5	8.7	2.3
Industry	. . .	103.9	78.5	66.2	80.4	37.5	23.2	12.8
Construction	. . .	. . .	64.1	37.5	39.4	16.0	26.4	−8.0
Transport and communications	. . .	. . .	89.5	30.1	91.2	19.6	29.7	12.4
Other	. . .	. . .	59.1	107.3	44.7	−14.0	5.7	1.1
(Share of NMP in constant 1986 prices)								
Net material product	100	100	100	100	100	100	100	100
Agriculture	80	60	53	44	36	36	34	33
Industry	14	19	24	28	35	40	43	45
Construction	. . .	7	8	7	7	7	8	7
Transport and communications	. . .	2	2	2	3	3	3	3
Other	. . .	12	13	19	19	14	12	12

Source: Statistical Directory, State Planning Commission.
[1]The figures in these tables are realized aggregate values for each five-year plan period.

during 1980–85 to no growth during 1985–90. Real GDP followed a similar path, growing by 1 percent during 1980–90, declining from 2 percent during 1980–85 to a marginal negative growth during 1985–90 (Table 4).[4] In addition to low growth, the 1980s were also characterized by wide yearly fluctuations in the level of output (Chart 2).

The stagnation in the 1980s is explained by various factors. First, despite relatively high (although declining) rates of investment in the economy, the marginal productivity of capital was almost negligible. Machinery and equipment, installed 20–40 years earlier, was used intensively and replaced infrequently, and by the 1980s was depleted in all sectors.[5]

Second, despite the emphasis on heavy industry and the paramount objective of self-sufficiency, growth continued to be highly dependent on external factors. Since the early 1960s Albania had relied heavily on Chinese assistance. The bulk of its imports of capital goods in the 1970s were of Chinese origin, largely financed by long-term credits. The constitutional ban on foreign credits in 1976 and the break with China in 1978 had a serious negative impact on the industrial sector and left some large projects uncompleted.

Third, the substantial variations in output around a negligible trend growth are largely explained by the agricultural sector's dependence on timely rainfall.[6] Adverse weather affects output in Albania in three ways. First, it directly impinges on the scale of agricultural output; second, given the strong linkages between agriculture and industry, it slows industrial production; and finally,

---

[4]The differences in the NMP and the GDP growth rates basically reflect the decline in growth of nonmaterial services from 1980–85 to 1985–90.

[5]Also, the ratio of NMP to gross output in the total material sphere remained largely unchanged at roughly 40 percent in the 1980s, indicating a stability in the aggregate input/output ratio, which, at largely unchanged prices in the 1980s, reflects the lack of technological improvements.

[6]The agricultural sector continues to be fairly important; it employs nearly 50 percent of the work force and contributed roughly 33 percent to NMP during 1980–90.

Table 4. Net Material Product and Gross Domestic Product by Final Use, 1980–90
(Summary indicators of output and expenditures)

	1980	1981	1982	1983	1984	1985	1986	1987	1988	1989	1990
					(In current prices)						
Net material product	12,862	13,265	13,625	13,696	13,300	13,602	14,013	13,700	13,631	15,223	13,229
Gross domestic product	15,538	16,074	16,544	16,724	16,510	16,863	17,390	17,254	17,008	18,681	16,234¹
					(In constant 1986 prices)						
Net material product	12,198	12,929	13,281	13,350	12,964	13,200	14,013	13,700	13,631	15,223	13,229
Gross domestic product	14,881	15,737	16,200	16,378	16,174	16,462	17,390	17,254	17,008	18,681	16,234¹
					(Annual percentage change in constant 1986 prices)						
Net material product	...	6.0	2.7	0.5	−2.9	1.8	6.2	−2.2	−0.5	11.7	−13.1
Personal consumption	...	1.9	0.8	6.6	2.5	0.8	4.6	3.4	1.1	6.9	2.0
Social consumption	...	2.7	1.9	3.3	2.7	0.4	0.4	3.1	−1.7	2.2	0.4
Total net investment	...	9.0	19.2	−13.6	−27.0	17.3	3.6	−17.0	13.3	30.6	−30.5
Net fixed investment	...	−8.6	19.9	2.5	−0.1	−13.8	6.6	5.1	3.1	10.9	−20.1
Gross domestic product	...	5.8	2.9	1.1	−1.2	1.8	5.6	−0.8	−1.4	9.8	−13.1
					(Share of NMP in constant 1986 prices)						
Personal consumption	62.6	60.1	59.0	62.6	66.1	65.4	64.4	68.1	69.2	66.3	77.8
Social consumption	10.8	10.4	10.4	10.6	11.3	11.1	10.5	11.1	10.9	10.0	11.6
Total net investment	25.2	25.9	30.1	25.8	19.4	22.4	21.8	18.5	21.1	24.7	19.8
Net fixed investment	24.4	21.1	24.6	25.0	25.8	21.8	21.9	23.5	24.4	24.2	22.3

Source: State Planning Commission.
¹IMF staff estimate.

Chart 2. Net Material Product and Gross Domestic Product, Annual Growth Rates, 1981–90
(In constant 1986 prices)

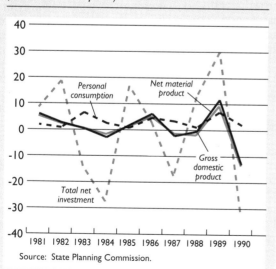

Source: State Planning Commission.

droughts cripple hydroelectric power stations, which provide over 90 percent of the electricity to the economy. As electricity has also been a significant export, its decline leads to a corresponding fall in Albania's imports, most of which have been machinery and equipment and scarce raw materials.

In 1990, the economy registered an unprecedented decline of over 13 percent in both NMP and GDP. It was an unusual year in that a very severe drought damaged almost all sectors of the economy—agriculture, agro-based industrial inputs, and exports. Moreover, the industrial sector was also subject to frequent power failures, and acute shortages in imported raw materials were caused by the curtailment of trade with Albania's major Central and East European trading partners. In addition, political turmoil and workers' dissatisfaction, accumulated over the years, finally manifested itself in strikes and labor unrest after mid-1990.

Changes in the composition of output during the 1980s have been erratic, reflecting shifts in the Government's investment priorities as well as the impact of weather. NMP in the agricultural sector

Chart 3. Sectoral Growth Rates, 1981–89

(In constant 1986 prices)

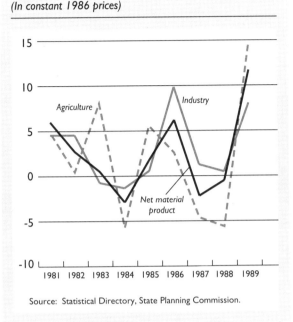

Source: Statistical Directory, State Planning Commission.

grew at an annual average rate of 2.1 percent during 1980–89 (Chart 3); data for 1990 by sector of origin are not available. The industrial sector expanded faster (averaging 3 percent a year) than the rest of the economy during 1980–89 (Table 3). Average annual growth rates of construction and building materials were negative, largely reflecting shortages of imported raw materials and capital goods during this period.

The share of agriculture in NMP during 1980–89 remained virtually constant at roughly 33 percent (Table 3). During the same period, industry represented nearly 44 percent, while the remainder was accounted for by construction (7.0 percent), transportation and communications (3.5 percent), and other. Within agriculture, the cooperative sector and private plots accounted for close to 70 percent; within the industrial sector, the share of heavy industry (including mining and energy) as a group was over 50 percent, while the largest share as a subgroup was in consumer goods—textiles, clothing, leather and food, beverages, and tobacco (roughly 10 percent each).

Expenditure

Domestic absorption—defined as the sum of personal consumption, social consumption, and investment—has on average been higher than NMP in the 1980s. In fact, in the second half of

the decade, it grew more rapidly than output, resulting in a sharp deterioration in Albania's net exports. The share of personal consumption in NMP rose sharply, from 60 percent in 1980 to 78 percent in 1990. The share of social consumption has, on average, remained constant at about 11 percent (with defense its main component), while that of net investment declined from 27 percent in 1980–85 to 21 percent in 1986–90 (Chart 4).

Variations in the composition of expenditure during 1980–90 were driven by large differences in the growth rates of its components: while consumption continued to grow, net investments receded. Personal consumption rose by 2.5 percent during 1980–85 and by 3.6 percent during 1985–90, while the growth of social consumption averaged 1.5 percent over the 1980s (Table 4). These increases in both personal and social real consumption were needed to maintain per capita consumption levels, given the high rates of population growth (nearly 2 percent a year during 1980–90). However, such high consumption growth relative to a stagnant output growth, in a setting of no capital inflows between 1979–89, implied a decline of total net investment. Total net investment fell at an annual average rate of 1.6 percent during 1980–90, worsening from a decline of 0.8 percent a year during 1980–85 to one of 2.4 percent in 1985–90 (Table 4). (For a more detailed discussion of investment, see below.)

Chart 4. Net Material Product by Final Use, 1980–90

(In millions of leks in constant 1986 prices)

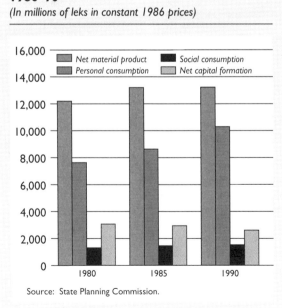

Source: State Planning Commission.

Table 5. Money Incomes and Expenditures of the Population in Current Prices, 1980–91
(In millions of leks)

	1980	1981	1982	1983	1984	1985	1986	1987	1988	1989	1990	Jan.–June 1990	Jan.–June 1991
Total money incomes	7,023	7,339	7,771	8,292	8,439	8,503	9,020	9,310	9,478	9,873	10,423	5,290	5,451
Wages	5,838	5,898	6,410	6,824	6,895	6,904	7,287	7,534	7,635	7,921	8,291	4,322	4,451
Social money benefits[1]	641	712	808	879	941	993	1,072	1,138	1,208	1,285	1,356	660	723
Nonwage incomes from economic activity[2]	218	225	135	144	158	170	159	188	237	267	363	127	117
Interest income	17	18	20	21	23	25	28	31	35	39	42	—	—
Bank credit for constructing private houses[3]	13	13	14	17	19	22	25	28	28	25	27	—	—
Other[4]	296	473	384	407	403	389	449	391	335	336	344	181	160
Total money expenditures	7,016	7,252	7,678	8,061	8,333	8,396	8,819	9,064	9,258	9,739	9,841	4,834	4,357
Retail purchases[5]	6,545	6,731	7,140	7,496	7,737	7,760	8,204	8,434	8,612	9,079	9,083	4,473	4,002
Services	333	353	357	367	379	389	396	418	440	452	469	229	187
Other													
Of which:	138	168	181	198	217	247	219	212	206	208	289	132	168
Taxes, levies, and transfers to government	4	5	5	5	6	6	6	6	6	6	6	...	...
Membership fees and subscriptions to specialized organizations[6]	22	23	26	26	27	28	29	29	34	30	30	...	...
Loans returned[7]	10	11	11	12	11	13	24	16	16	18	18	...	...
Other	12	129	139	155	173	200	160	161	150	154	235	...	...
Financial savings (including new loans)	7	87	93	231	106	107	201	246	220	134	582	456	1,094
Cash	32	52	35	128	12	22	89	101	71	46	441	319	237
Bank deposits	39	35	58	103	94	85	112	145	149	88	141	137	857
Memorandum item:													
Savings ratio (as a percentage of total money incomes)	0.1	1.2	1.2	2.8	1.3	1.3	2.2	2.6	2.3	1.4	5.6	8.6	20.1

Source: State Planning Commission.
[1]Differences between social money benefits in this table and social security expenditures in the fiscal tables are accounted for by expenditures on administrative costs and some noncash benefits such as health institutions for children.
[2]Includes some private activity, a substantial part of which is incomes earned from collecting herbs for medicinal purposes.
[3]These constitute the borrowings of the population and are included in total money incomes.
[4]Includes transfers from relatives abroad, for official travel, and from lectures and conferences.
[5]Includes expenditures on housing construction, which are instead excluded from circulation of retail trade in Table 11.
[6]Includes social and political organizations.
[7]Includes interest payments on loans.

Household Income, Saving, and Consumption

The primary sources of income of the population (including loans) are wages, social money benefits, and nonwage incomes from some small private economic activities. In 1989 (for which data are relatively more reliable), wages accounted for 80 percent of the money incomes, while social money benefits and nonwage incomes were 13 percent and 4 percent, respectively (Table 5).

Given low rates of interest and limits on bank credit to the private sector during the 1980s, interest income and loans were negligible. Interest income, however, has tripled since the beginning of the 1980s, reflecting involuntary increases in savings, mainly in the form of deposits, resulting from shortages of consumer goods and the absence of other saving instruments. Personal loans were extended only to cooperative members for constructing houses in rural areas; in fact, outstanding loans for urban dwellings declined in the 1980s. Recent changes in housing loan policy broaden access to bank credit, but downpayment terms make less than 5 percent of the population eligible (for details, see Section V).

During 1980–89, the savings ratio averaged 1.6 percent (Table 5); this ratio increased to 5.6 percent in 1990, reflecting increases in consumer goods shortages (the striking jump in the savings

Chart 5. Money Incomes and Expenditures of Population, 1980–90

(In millions of leks)

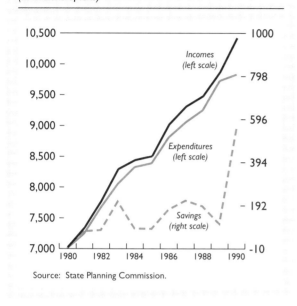

Source: State Planning Commission.

ratio in 1990 is evident in Chart 5). This ratio continued to rise during 1991 (from 8.6 percent in the first half of 1990 to 20.1 percent in the corresponding period of 1991) as a result of wage increases and declines in retail purchases. The declines in retail purchases have clearly been involuntary and result directly from the collapse of production and the shortages of imported goods in 1991.

Sectoral Developments

Agriculture

By the end of the 1980s, Albania's agricultural sector constituted roughly 33 percent of NMP and employed nearly 50 percent of the total working population, of which 80 percent were in the cooperative sector. The total area of arable land remained virtually unchanged in the 1980s, with state farms owning roughly 22 percent of the land and contributing 28 percent to output; the corresponding figures for the cooperative sector were 75 percent and 61 percent. The rest was accounted for by small plot holders belonging to the cooperatives cultivating primarily for their own consumption. Output per hectare in private plots was far higher than that of the state or the cooperative farms. Cooperatives produced mainly cereals (75 percent of total cereal production), rice (100 percent), tobacco (100 percent), and livestock; the

state farms, located closer to the populated areas, produced mainly fruits and vegetables, which constitute Albania's major agricultural export items.

Management and Organization. The management system of state farms was modeled after the Soviet *soukhozes*. Even though large shareholdings were confiscated to establish these farms, over 95 percent of the state farms have been settled on new land, reclaimed through substantial investment in land improvement during the 1950s and the 1960s. Arable land expanded by more than 250 percent over the first 20 years through land reclamation, extension of irrigation and electricity services, and soil improvement programs. Currently, state farms operate in the most productive areas of the country. They have been dependent on the state budget for their investment, wage fund, and working capital requirements, and have had to meet prespecified production targets. Under the reforms introduced since mid-1990, investment financing by the state budget has been almost eliminated, except for large projects such as irrigation.

Cooperatives, on the other hand, were organized through forcible consolidation of private holdings. They have also been highly dependent on state institutions: they lease machinery and equipment from the state-owned machine and tractor stations; obtain most of their inputs from state enterprises; and sell their produce to state entities according to centrally planned targets and at fixed prices. But they have predominantly self-financed their investments and most of their working capital, paid profit taxes, and followed an independent wage policy depending on the internal generation of profits. Average wages in the state farms have consistently been nearly double those in the cooperative sector.

State farms and cooperatives have been typically very large, and, to alleviate the diseconomies of large-scale management, many have been split into smaller units in the past two years; by the end of 1990, the total number of state farms had increased from 70 to 120, and cooperatives from 420 to more than 1,000. Some additional agrarian reforms were also implemented in the first quarter of 1991, including the introduction of private plots (0.2 hectares) for state farm workers and the doubling of the private plots (from 0.2 to 0.4 hectares) for cooperative members, who were also permitted to buy livestock from their cooperatives. As of mid-1991, however, there was evidence of large-scale spontaneous dismantling of the cooperative system and the distribution of cooperative land and livestock among its members.

Output and Investment. Agricultural output has largely depended on weather and has therefore varied widely from year to year. Although the

Table 6. Agricultural Production and Pattern of Ownership, 1980–90

	1980	1981	1982	1983	1984	1985	1986	1987	1988	1989	1990
	(In millions of leks at current prices)										
Total gross agricultural production	6,894	7,012	7,291	7,975	7,535	7,821	8,402	8,441	7,921	8,772	8,120
Crop production	3,940	4,153	4,427	4,844	4,465	4,696	5,080	4,995	4,423	4,795	4,071
Fruits and olives	565	589	611	691	556	578	539	572	537	602	516
Livestock	2,069	1,971	1,960	2,117	2,186	2,204	2,456	2,571	2,616	2,807	2,963
Forestry and related activities	320	299	293	323	328	343	327	303	345	568	570
	(In millions of leks at constant 1986 prices)										
Total gross agricultural production	6,987	7,245	7,533	8,240	7,785	8,081	8,402	8,441	7,921	8,772	8,120
Crop production	3,946	4,278	4,562	4,992	4,597	4,837	5,080	4,995	4,423	4,795	4,071
Fruits and olives	548	589	611	691	556	578	539	572	537	602	516
Livestock	2,180	2,079	2,067	2,234	2,304	2,323	2,456	2,571	2,616	2,807	2,963
Forestry and related activities	313	299	293	323	328	343	327	303	345	568	570
	(Share of total production at constant 1986 prices)										
Total gross agricultural production	100	100	100	100	100	100	100	100	100	100	. . .
State farms	25	25	27	26	29	28	30	30	30	30	. . .
Cooperatives	56	59	62	65	62	63	62	61	60	60	. . .
Private plots	19	16	12	9	9	9	9	9	9	10	. . .
	(In thousands of hectares)										
Area of agricultural land	702.0	705.9	708.6	709.8	711.2	712.7	712.8	714.0	714.2	706.2	. . .
	(Share of total land ownership)										
Area of agricultural land	100	100	100	100	100	100	100	100	100	100	. . .
State farms	21	21	21	22	22	23	23	23	23	24	. . .
Cooperatives	76	76	76	76	75	75	74	74	74	74	. . .
Private plots	3	3	3	3	3	3	3	3	3	3	. . .

Source: State Planning Commission.

irrigation system with its feeder canals now extends to nearly 60 percent of the arable land, insufficient reservoirs have prevented its full capacity from being utilized, and the economy continues to depend on timely rainfall.

Since the early 1950s, agriculture has received less support than industry, and, within agriculture, industrial crops such as cotton, tobacco, sugar beets, and sunflower were favored at the expense of foodgrain and livestock production. Although the plans repeatedly emphasized the importance of increasing the output of foodgrains such as wheat, rye, and oatmeal, the objective of attaining self-sufficiency in food production was rarely achieved and food has been intermittently imported. Also, livestock production was hampered by a perpetual shortage of fodder that resulted, in part, from the diversion of meadows and pastures to crop production. Crops constitute the bulk of agricultural output, averaging 58 percent of total production during 1980–90, followed by livestock (30 percent) and fruits (7 percent). Within crop production, grain, maize, vegetables, and tobacco are the most

significant, while cattle and pork meat and milk are among the important livestock products.

One characteristic feature of the agricultural sector in 1980–90 was the dramatic yearly changes in output, reflecting not only weather but also an erratic investment pattern during the period. The real growth of gross agricultural output during 1980–89 averaged 2.6 percent annually. Livestock production grew at much higher rates than crop and fruit production (Table 6). Gross agricultural output fell by an unprecedented 7.4 percent in 1990, largely on account of crop and fruit production. Poor performance was mainly accounted for by a severe drought, acute shortages of domestic and imported raw materials, and, as in other sectors, work disruptions during political turmoil.

Investment rates in the agricultural sector varied widely during the 1980s; growth in net capital formation ranged from declines of over 20 percent (1987) to increases of 32 percent (1989), averaging an annual rate of 5.5 percent between 1980 and 1989. Most of the investment was directed to the extension of irrigation facilities and farm

Table 7. Comparison of Agricultural Productivity Among East European Countries, 1988

	Albania	Bulgaria	Czechoslovakia	Hungary	Poland	Romania
	(In tons per hectare)					
Wheat	3.20	4.01	5.28	5.45	3.48	3.58
Potatoes	5.41	9.73	20.64	. . .	18.60	. . .
Sunflower seeds	0.70	1.57	. . .	. . .	. . .	1.51
Sugar beets	17.19	16.08	18.60	39.34	34.13	11.36
Milk yield per cow (in liters)	1,274	3,397	3,777	. . .	. . .	2,074
Eggs per chicken	96	170	247	. . .	. . .	154

Sources: Data provided by the authorities; and IMF staff estimates.

mechanization. The fluctuations in state farms' investments are indicative of the shifts in the Government's priorities and also reflect large projects and capital imports in given years. In contrast, the erratic growth of capital formation in the cooperative sector was basically driven by the performance of agricultural output, as cooperatives have largely used their own resources for making investments.

Data on agricultural exports and imports indicate that the food situation eased in the 1980s. The balance of trade in food items was positive on average, but negative in agricultural raw materials. The severing of relationships with China in 1978 hampered the pace of agricultural mechanization; Chinese tractors and harvest combines could not be easily replaced, and therefore imports of such equipment were negligible in the 1980s until 1989.

A cross-country comparison of agricultural productivity in 1988 indicates that in virtually all comparable products, Albania's performance was the poorest among the East European countries (Table 7 and Chart 6). Moreover, the stagnation in productivity is also apparent across time in crops, fruit, and livestock (Table 8). Productivity in nearly all categories of crops, fruit, and livestock was higher in state farms than in cooperative farms, as the state sector owns the most productive land and has easier access to infrastructure.

Industry

The industrial sector in Albania includes the branches of mining, manufacturing, and energy production. At present, Albania has a broad industrial base, which (except for metal and mineral production) reflects the pursuit of autarkic policies more than the economy's comparative advantage. Albania produces a very large proportion of its

industrial consumption and spare parts for its equipment, but frequently at high cost and with low quality. In 1990, industry accounted for approximately 45 percent of NMP, absorbed 42 percent of gross investment, and provided employment for about 23 percent of the working population.

Structure and Organization. Albanian enterprises have been production units with extremely limited financial and managerial autonomy, directly attached to the Government through their respective ministries and subject to strict plan tar-

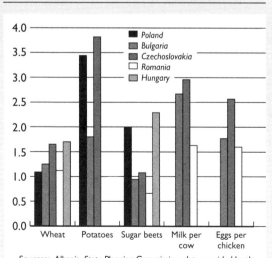

Chart 6. Comparison of Agricultural Productivity Among East European Countries[1]

Sources: Albania, State Planning Commission; data provided by the authorities; and IMF staff estimates for other East European countries.
[1] A value of unity indicates the same productivity in Albania and other East European countries. A value greater (lesser) than unity indicates higher (lower) productivity in other East European countries.

Table 8. Area Under Cultivation, Production, and Yields of Selected Agricultural Products, 1980–90

	1980	1981	1982	1983	1984	1985	1986	1987	1988	1989	1990
					(Quintals per hectare)[1]						
Wheat	25.3	25.2	26.9	30.9	28.7	31.4	28.9	31.1	32.0	29.3	29.1
Maize	27.9	34.0	37.3	41.4	36.4	35.0	44.9	37.7	32.9	47.9	32.4
Rice	30.8	34.8	29.5	33.9	32.2	33.6	33.0	31.8	27.2	31.3	20.0
Potatoes	60.6	71.7	64.9	94.3	70.9	57.2	78.6	61.0	54.1	99.7	39.5
Vegetables and melon	137.2	139.2	151.3	155.6	153.1	161.4	168.8	168.6	138.9	175.1	140.9
Dried beans	7.4	9.1	5.8	11.5	5.3	8.8	11.3	6.9	9.9	10.0	4.1
Tobacco	6.4	8.3	8.6	7.5	8.6	8.7	8.3	7.8	4.7	7.1	5.3
Sunflower	11.0	11.1	10.9	15.8	9.0	10.9	11.8	9.0	7.0	11.3	6.9
Cotton	7.7	9.9	10.5	9.0	14.1	17.7	16.7	16.0	10.0	14.7	9.8
Sugar beet	277.4	320.4	347.0	391.1	300.0	272.1	243.7	249.6	171.9	397.1	255.1
					(Yield in kilograms per root)						
Apples, pears, peaches, figs	11.7	15.3	14	15.3	11.8	9.5	11.0	9.7	9.3	11.3	9.0
Grapes (in quintals)[1]	36.9	36.6	43.7	43.4	36.0	34.2	25.8	30.1	24.0	24.0	18.0
Olives	12.8	10.9	7.5	20.3	3.1	12.1	6.3	12.4	6.9	9.2	3.5
Citrus fruits	21.1	16.5	21.4	21.7	19.0	19.0	18.4	13.2	16.9	20.3	14.0
					(Yield per unit)						
Average live weight (kg)											
Slaughtered cattle	162.3	150.3	149.7	170.4	179.0	172.3	170.7	168.2	141.8	151.7	148.0
Slaughtered pigs	62.4	64.8	68.1	71.1	75.5	69.3	68.4	65.8	53.6	59.4	56.3
Average annual milk yield/cow (liters)	1,327	1,228	1,258	1,377	1,447	1,318	1,301	1,309	1,274	1,276	1,466
Average annual egg production/chicken	82.0	84.0	88.0	92.0	98.0	98.0	101.0	103.0	96.0	98.0	99.0
Number of calves born per 100 cows	83.0	78.0	86.0	88.0	80.0	83.0	80.0	77.0	83.0	83.0	83.0
Number of piglets born per sow	8.0	8.0	9.0	10.0	12.0	11.0	11.0	11.0	9.0	10.0	9.0

Source: State Planning Commission.
[1] One quintal = 100 kilograms.

gets. In 1990, the plethora of quantitative targets was largely replaced by the single criterion of profit, and managers have been given some discretion in deciding the use of a small proportion of productive capacity once state orders have been fulfilled. However, most enterprises could not take advantage of the reforms because they faced financial constraints and had limited access to local and imported inputs, lack of spare capacity, and other limitations that inhibited their ability to increase production.

Output Trends. Starting from a very small industrial base after the Second World War, the Government embarked on a very ambitious plan of rapid industrialization. Despite its quest for self-reliance and autarky, Albania had to depend heavily on the U.S.S.R. and China as sources of technology and development assistance, and the pace of industrial development has been closely correlated to the scale of foreign assistance.

Between 1950 and 1975, in response to high rates of investment, total industrial output grew rapidly, averaging more than 10 percent a year. By 1980, however, industrial growth rates had decelerated substantially, and between 1980 and 1989 industrial production grew at less than 3 percent a year in real terms, and fell by 7.5 percent in 1990, when production in most industries, particularly capital goods, fell below the 1985 levels (Table 9).

Developments in capital and consumer goods industries generally reflect rigid government policies during the past forty years. Until 1965, capital and consumer goods industries developed at a similar pace, and on several occasions the Government reallocated investments in order to maintain growth of consumer goods production. However, in the 1970s, the development strategy was switched radically to emphasize capital goods and heavy industries. As a result, growth rates of capital and consumer goods diverged, with the most rapid increases being registered in chemicals, copper mining and processing, engineering, and

Table 9. Industrial Production, 1980–90

	1980	1981	1982	1983	1984	1985	1986	1987	1988	1989	1990
	(In millions of leks at current prices)										
Total gross output	15,314	15,842	16,516	16,650	17,082	16,890	16,891	17,141	17,497	18,370	16,996
Capital goods	9,796	10,227	10,560	10,553	10,950	10,773	10,951	10,956	11,177	11,574	10,237
Consumer goods	5,518	5,615	5,956	6,097	6,132	6,117	5,940	6,185	6,320	6,796	6,759
Energy	2,068	1,812	1,694	1,365	1,429	1,337	1,474	1,385	1,371	1,394	1,267
Mining	1,406	1,788	1,883	2,049	2,203	2,051	2,360	2,442	2,683	2,812	2,181
Manufacturing	11,840	12,242	12,939	13,236	13,450	13,502	13,057	13,314	13,443	14,164	13,548
	(In millions of leks at 1986 constant prices)										
Total gross output	14,145	15,085	15,724	15,851	16,262	16,082	16,891	17,141	17,497	18,370	16,996
Capital goods	9,024	9,705	10,014	10,015	10,387	10,224	10,951	10,956	11,177	11,574	10,237
Consumer goods	5,121	5,380	5,710	5,836	5,875	5,858	5,940	6,185	6,320	6,796	6,759
Energy	1,700	1,748	1,639	1,312	1,359	1,276	1,474	1,385	1,371	1,394	1,267
Mining	1,661	1,893	1,993	2,159	2,330	2,187	2,360	2,442	2,683	2,812	2,181
Manufacturing	10,784	11,444	12,092	12,380	12,573	12,619	13,057	13,314	13,443	14,164	13,548
	(Share of total production at 1986 constant prices)										
Total gross output	100	100	100	100	100	100	100	100	100	100	100
Capital goods	64	64	64	63	64	64	65	64	64	63	60
Consumer goods	36	36	36	37	36	36	35	36	36	37	40
Energy	12	12	10	8	8	8	9	8	8	8	7
Mining	12	13	13	14	14	14	14	14	15	15	13
Manufacturing	76	76	77	78	77	78	77	78	77	77	80

Source: State Planning Commission.

power generation. But from 1975, the growth rates of producer and consumer goods industries were again similar, largely as a result of the ban on external assistance, with severe declines recorded in heavy industry. In spite of the emphasis on heavy industry, light and food industries still represent more than 35 percent of total industrial production.

Mining. Albania is endowed with a wide range of metals and minerals, including chromium, copper, iron/nickel, coal/lignite, bauxite, phosphorate, asbestos, bituminous sands, pyrites and nickel silicate, as well as limestone, sands, marble, and clays. In 1990, the mining industry accounted for approximately 14 percent of gross industrial production in terms of domestic prices and for a substantial share of export earnings. Disaggregated trends in metal and mineral production are summarized in Appendix Table A4.

The most significant metal resource is *chromium.* Albania is the world's third largest producer of chromium ore, after the former U.S.S.R. and South Africa. Geological reserves of chromium amount to 37 million tons, of which 22 million

tons are considered exploitable.[7] Despite substantial reserves, increases in ore production have been minimal during the 1980s as a result of declining productivity of existing mines, poor transportation facilities, and difficulties in opening new mines, owing to the lack of investment funds. In addition, the relatively stable level of ore output over the past decade conceals unfavorable trends in the industry, in particular a significant decline in the share of high-content ore, and an inability to increase the amount of processing into concentrate and ferrochrome, the major chromium export products along with high-content ore.

Albania has some 50 million tons of *copper* reserves, but average copper content (between 1.5 and 3 percent) is low by international mining standards. Mines with higher ore content are rapidly being exhausted, and many new mines are produc-

---

[7]Reserves are being added at an annual rate of 3 million tons, but in recent years the Department of Geological Survey has had little success in locating new reserves of high-content chromium because of inadequate equipment and exploration technology.

ing low-content ore, largely owing to the lack of equipment and exploration technology capable of locating high-content deposits. Low output growth in the late 1980s has largely resulted from inadequate mechanization and deteriorating mining conditions. Albania has developed its own processing plants based on Chinese designs for concentrating copper ore and producing copper wire, which is the main export commodity.

Albania has approximately 270 million tons of geological reserves of *iron/nickel* ore, about two thirds of which is believed to be minable. The country's reserves of *lignite* are large and are estimated at roughly 700 million tons of geological reserves and 150 million tons of minable deposits. This sector is characterized by difficult mining conditions (uneven and thin strata), and much of the mined lignite has high ash and impurity contents. Currently, many lignite mines are operating at a loss.

Energy. In addition to eight small-capacity thermal power stations (old and with poor conversion efficiencies), Albania has substantial *electricity* generating capacity from hydroelectric power. The periods of high growth in production of hydroelectric power were in the 1960s and between 1975 and 1980, reflecting the completion of various major production facilities. Electricity sales to neighboring countries (made through grid connections with Yugoslavia and Greece) have been a very important export. Since 1987, modest water flows have reduced annual output, and a severe drought in 1990 reduced electricity generation by nearly 30 percent and crippled the whole economy, including its exports.

Reserves of *oil and gas* have supplied domestic petroleum product needs and raw materials for the chemical industry. Oil production peaked in 1974 at 2.25 million tons and gas production peaked in 1982 at 940 million cubic meters. Since then, oil production has fallen steadily to less than 1.1 million tons, and gas output has fallen rapidly to little more than 200 million cubic meters, as existing wells have been exhausted and attempts to locate new reserves unsuccessful. Given the unwillingness to seek external assistance and technology for exploration and recovery, a large amount of investment (about $500 million, or 25 percent of total industrial investment in the past decade) has been wasted, because no new commercially viable reserves have been found. All the domestically produced oil is now processed by local refineries.

In recent years, small amounts of crude oil have been imported, and imports of final products have been financed by exports of other products (such as bitumen) from Albanian refineries. In fact, over

the past decade, the trade surplus in energy products was steadily eroded, and in physical terms Albania became a net importer of total energy in 1988, with all the deficit incurred in its convertible currency trade. In value terms, it became a net importer a few years earlier.

Manufacturing. Manufacturing constitutes the largest part of the overall industrial sector (Table 9), representing approximately 80 percent of total industrial production in 1990. During the past decade, manufacturing output has grown at an annual average rate of less than 3 percent. Virtually all branches of manufacturing experienced substantial variation in annual growth rates, but the overall structure of output changed only slightly. In 1990, when industrial output fell by 7.5 percent, the most substantial declines were concentrated in heavy industries (more than 11 percent). Consumer goods industries were much less affected (with a decline of less than 1 percent), partly because of significant increases in foreign exchange allocations for importing inputs. However, in the first half of 1991, provisional data suggest that food and light industries are experiencing disproportionately large falls in output, and more than one third of light industry enterprises have had to suspend operations, largely because of shortages of domestic and imported inputs. However, other sectors have also continued to fare badly, and as Table A4 indicates, there are some industries whose January–June 1991 production has been more than half the 1990 level.

Food and light industries remain the largest branches of manufacturing, accounting for 28 percent and 20 percent, respectively, of total industrial production in 1990. Milling, bakeries, and pasta production are the most important branches of the *food industry*, together accounting for about 50 percent of its output. Currently, food industries account for only 10 percent of exports. Many of the processing plants need modernization, particularly to improve quality and packaging for export.

Light industry is based predominantly on imported raw materials and geared largely to meeting domestic needs. The main branches (textiles, knitting, and clothing) account for half the value of sectoral production. Production has been adversely influenced in recent years by shortages of imported inputs more than by productive capacity constraints, but much of the capital equipment is now reaching the limits of its productive age. Cigarettes and textiles are the only light industries with significant exports.

Heavy industry represents about 31 percent of total industrial output, reflecting the past emphasis on promoting capital goods industries and self-sufficiency in spare parts. The larger components are electrical products and a wide range of spare parts for industry, transport, mining, and agriculture. Engineering enterprises also produce consumer goods, such as electrical appliances, televisions, and radios. Production is largely based on local designs and imported licenses, and modernization of technology and equipment is again urgently needed.

The other main branches of heavy industry are chemicals, building materials, timber, and paper products, each of which in 1990 accounted for about 5 percent of total industrial production. The main chemical products are nitrogenous and phosphatic fertilizers, pesticides, and a range of simple basic chemicals for domestic needs. Because of shortages of gas and imported spare parts and inputs, production has declined in recent years, particularly in fertilizers; as of June 1991, all fertilizer factories were idle.

Construction and Housing

Construction. Construction activity played an important role, particularly during 1950–75, in meeting the ambitious targets of heavy industry investments, rural electrification, and irrigation systems and mining, as well as in providing housing for a rapidly growing population. The pace of growth has, however, been erratic and the quality of work poor. Owing to its dependence on imported inputs and foreign assistance, the pace of construction activity slowed and a number of projects had to be abandoned after 1978.

Outmoded technology and depletion of the capital stock are, as in other sectors, also apparent in the construction sector. Transportation and construction equipment and machinery are between 20–30 years old, have been poorly maintained, and are energy inefficient. Inadequate investment funds and shortages of raw materials have been reflected in the insufficient provision of infrastructural facilities. There are few paved roads, and the railway system is not only outdated but the lines connect only a few major cities. Electricity was an exception, and by 1971, it was available to all urban and rural areas.

During the 1950s, the former U.S.S.R. financed the construction of hydroelectric power stations and textile and sugar mills. After 1961, Chinese foreign aid was significant in financing major mining projects in copper, chromium, and ferronickel, an oil refinery, and also cement mills and steel plants. A number of construction projects, initiated before the break with China in 1978, could not be completed thereafter.

As in the rest of the economy, there was a marked slowdown in construction activity in the 1980s. Gross output in construction increased marginally by an annual average rate of 0.7 percent during 1980–89 (Table 10). The share of construction in NMP averaged roughly 7 percent during the same period. Official estimates for 1989–90 suggest a sharp fall by 14.7 percent in investment construction, primarily owing to a shortage of imported and domestic inputs. Gross output in construction is estimated to have declined by over 25 percent in the first quarter of 1991 compared with the corresponding period of the previous year.

The composition of construction activity during 1980–89 indicates that, although the share of investment construction had declined during this period, it still accounted for more than 50 percent of the total in 1989. There was a corresponding rise in the share of research in oil exploration (which is considered part of construction activity in the Albanian system), from 21 percent in 1980 to 29 percent in 1989.

Housing. Most urban housing in Albania is owned and financed by the state, whereas housing in rural areas is private and predominantly owner financed. (Some housing units constructed before World War II in urban areas continue to be privately owned, however.) While in the cities housing construction has been centrally planned and implemented, in rural areas it was decided individually, and rural workers could obtain limited financial assistance from their cooperatives.

Although rent on state-owned houses has been fixed, at low rates, and generally ranges from 6–10 percent of the renter's monthly income, monthly expenditure on housing, including utility costs, reaches 20–25 percent. State rent revenues, excluding utilities, have been allocated mostly to cover repairs and maintenance but most government-owned houses are of low quality and have been poorly maintained.

Demand for housing in both rural and urban areas has far exceeded supply. During the 1980s, housing construction remained virtually unchanged (Table 10), despite widespread shortages and the rapid growth of the population. The share of housing in gross output of the construction sector averaged only 4 percent during 1980–89. Criteria for renting state-owned houses establish that the space allocated per person should average 4–6 square meters. Currently, there are 200 apartments per 1,000 inhabitants in the cities, compared with 288 required to meet the norms. According to the estimates made by local authorities, roughly 55,000 additional apartments would be needed to fulfill the norms. To cope with the excess demand,

Table 10. Construction Activity, 1980–89

	1980	1981	1982	1983	1984	1985	1986	1987	1988	1989
				(In millions of leks at current prices)						
Total gross output	2,865	2,979	3,264	3,248	3,225	2,986	2,861	2,817	2,851	3,060
Material inputs	1,974	2,040	2,223	2,178	2,160	2,007	1,925	1,938	1,960	2,071
Net material product	891	939	1,041	1,070	1,065	979	936	879	891	989
				(In millions of leks at constant 1986 prices)						
Total gross output	2,945	2,856	3,130	3,114	3,092	2,864	2,861	2,817	2,851	3,060
Material inputs	2,131	1,944	2,119	2,075	2,057	1,912	1,925	1,938	1,960	2,071
Net material product	814	912	1,011	1,039	1,035	952	936	879	891	989
				(Share of total gross output at constant 1986 prices)						
Total gross output	100.0	100.0	100.0	100.0	100.0	100.0	100.0	100.0	100.0	100.0
Investment construction[1]	61.8	60.1	57.7	57.1	55.9	54.1	52.7	54.1	52.2	52.5
Of which:										
State enterprises	34.0	32.6	32.7	33.7	33.4	31.2	29.8	32.8	32.0	32.1
State farms[2,3]	7.3	9.7	9.9	10.2	9.3	8.4	8.4	8.2	8.2	8.1
Agricultural cooperatives[3]	3.5	6.7	5.0	3.9	3.8	4.4	5.0	3.6	3.2	3.6
Social organizations[4]	0.9	0.8	1.7	1.7	1.6	2.6	2.6	2.7	2.4	2.6
Other[5]	16.1	10.3	8.4	7.5	7.8	7.4	6.9	6.9	6.6	6.2
Repairs and maintenance	4.9	5.4	5.6	5.7	5.8	6.5	6.9	7.3	7.4	7.4
Research in oil exploration	20.9	21.1	22.3	22.6	24.6	25.8	28.8	27.3	29.6	29.0
Land improvement	5.9	6.1	7.5	7.2	6.5	6.1	4.9	4.3	4.1	4.0
Studies and projections	1.4	1.7	1.7	1.7	1.7	1.6	1.4	1.6	1.5	1.7
Housing	3.8	4.1	3.7	4.2	3.9	4.2	3.5	3.5	3.4	3.7
Other	1.3	1.5	1.5	1.5	1.6	1.8	1.8	1.8	1.8	1.7
				(Annual percentage change at constant 1986 prices)						
Total gross output		−3.0	9.6	−0.5	−0.7	−7.4	−0.1	−1.5	1.2	7.3
Investment construction[1]		−5.6	5.2	−1.6	−2.8	−10.4	−2.6	1.0	−2.2	8.0
Of which:										
State enterprises		−7.2	10.2	2.4	−1.7	−13.4	−4.7	8.5	−1.4	7.9
State farms[2,3]		29.3	11.5	2.9	−9.7	−16.3	−0.4	−4.2	1.3	6.0
Agricultural cooperatives[3]		88.2	−19.3	−20.6	−4.1	6.8	14.3	−29.9	−10.9	21.1
Social organizations[4]		−11.1	116.7	1.9	−5.7	48.0	1.4	—	−10.7	17.9
Other[5]		−38.1	−9.9	−11.7	3.0	−11.3	−7.5	−2.0	−2.6	1.1
Repairs and maintenance		6.2	13.6	0.6	1.7	4.5	4.8	4.6	2.4	7.6
Research in oil exploration		−2.0	15.6	1.0	8.1	−3.0	11.7	−6.6	9.5	5.1
Land improvement		—	35.6	−5.5	−10.3	−12.5	−20.0	−12.9	−4.9	5.2
Studies and projections		17.1	10.4	—	−1.9	−13.5	−8.9	12.2	−4.3	18.2
Housing		4.4	−2.5	14.8	−7.6	−1.6	−15.8	−2.0	−1.0	16.3
Other		10.5	14.3	—	4.2	2.0	—	2.0	−1.9	2.0

Sources: Department of Statistics, State Planning Commission; and Ministry of Construction.
[1] Investment in construction consists of all investment expenditures excluding machinery and equipment.
[2] Includes production of crops, water, forestry, and others.
[3] Includes irrigation projects.
[4] Includes women, youth, professional, and party organizations.
[5] Includes education, health, and military.

industrial state enterprises have often been encouraged to provide housing for their employees. In effect, with budgetary support and under the supervision of these state enterprises, the employees often construct their houses themselves without being remunerated for their services.

In mid-1990, policies to encourage construction of private housing in urban areas were introduced. Residents are eligible for bank credit, repayable over five years, up to 50 percent of the total value of the house. However, with relatively high construction costs and the current levels of income and savings, it is still virtually impossible for the majority of the population to construct a house.

Internal Trading Activity

Until the mid-1990 reforms, internal trade, both wholesale and retail, was state controlled. Consumer goods were distributed by the state through the store outlets of internal trading state enterprises and, to a limited extent, by the cooperatives. The share of consumer goods distributed by the cooperatives averaged 14 percent during 1980–90.

Structure and Organization. There were 125 state-controlled internal trading enterprises before mid-1990, which distributed retail goods throughout the country. In cities, trading enterprises were differentiated according to the kinds of goods they distributed—foodstuffs or industrial goods—while smaller towns and villages were served by cooperatives and nonspecialized trading enterprises.

All state trading enterprises receive directives from the central planning authorities about the retail prices and the quantities to be sold. To achieve their distribution targets, the trading enterprises contract with the industrial enterprises and with the *grumbullims* (the specialized state organizations responsible for collecting agricultural products). However, fruits and vegetables are purchased direct from state farms and cooperatives by the internal trading enterprises to reduce waste and spoilage.

Retail prices of nearly all commodities (except fruit and vegetables) have remained unchanged since the late 1960s. Industrial enterprises sell to trading enterprises at prices that cover wholesale prices and the turnover taxes. When retail prices were lower than wholesale prices plus the turnover tax, the losses of the internal trading enterprises were directly subsidized by the budget.[8] However, it is apparent that, in the aggregate, the internal trading enterprises have been profitable (Table 11).[9] In 1990, the profits of the trading enterprises declined by an unprecedented 35 percent, owing to wage increases and to riots in the second half of the year that severely damaged some retail stores.

Since August 1990, private activity in internal trade has been allowed in services such as restaurants, sales of fruits, vegetables, and meat, and some areas of commerce. The growth of private trading is reflected in an increase of nearly 9 percent in the total number of shops and stores in the country in less than a year, compared with an average annual growth in the past decade of less than 2 percent. Also, there has been an attempt to split internal trading enterprises into smaller units to encourage specialization.

Trends. Total turnover of goods increased by an annual average of nearly 3 percent during 1980–90. However, goods sold by internal trading enterprises declined markedly (minus 12.8 percent) in the first half of 1991, compared with the corresponding period of 1990, on account of severe supply constraints, which also caused a depletion of stock by almost 30 percent.

Rationing of consumer goods has not been uncommon in Albania. In periods of rationing, each family is assigned specified quantities of food items such as sugar, rice, oil, butter, cheese, and beans. The system of rationing has not been evenly practiced throughout the country; each of the districts, with the exception of Tirana, was expected to satisfy local requirements. Even though shortages have been frequent and have sporadically resulted in the emergence of black markets, the associated penalties have limited their size, and no organized unofficial market has been tolerated.

Data on "excess demand registered at retail stores"—the value of all commodities in current prices demanded by consumers visiting the retail stores but not available during that year—show that during 1980–90 excess demand increased by an average of 9 percent annually (Table 11). This figure, in fact, may underestimate actual excess demand, since consumers may fail to register their preferences when they know from experience that the desired goods are not available. An interesting picture that emerges from Table 11 is the coexistence of a substantial stock of unsold goods, averaging 33 percent of total goods sold during 1980–90, along with increasing excess demand during 1980–90. This phenomenon clearly points to mismatches between supply and demand owing to relative price distortions. As a result, during the 1980s, not only was demand growing faster than supply in the aggregate, but also the product mix was inappropriate to satisfy existing and emerging demand.

Concurrent with the dismantling of the cooperative sector in 1991, there was a decline in the share of products distributed through the state-controlled *grumbullims* (roughly 50 percent in the first half of 1991 on a year-on-year basis). Private plot holders had begun to divert larger proportions of their output to private markets in response to higher prices. There also appeared to be increasing evidence of hoarding for self-consumption. Owing to large-scale bottlenecks in private transportation and refrigeration, foodstuffs in urban areas were becoming increasingly scarce.

---

[8]See below for a detailed discussion of the relationship between procurement, wholesale, and retail prices.

[9]Budgetary subsidies on agricultural commodities have generally been paid to the *grumbullims*.

Table 11. Internal Trading Activity in Current Prices, 1980–91

	1980	1981	1982	1983	1984	1985	1986	1987	1988	1989	1990	Jan.–June 1990	Jan.–June 1991
							(In millions of leks)						
Total circulation of goods	6,577	6,761	7,133	7,474	7,666	7,679	8,097	8,315	8,373	8,768	8,694	—	—
Circulation of goods by cooperatives	883	916	1,008	1,050	1,081	1,129	1,134	1,143	1,168	1,232	1,116	—	—
Goods sold by internal trading enterprises	5,694	5,845	6,125	6,424	6,585	6,550	6,963	7,172	7,205	7,536	7,578	3,755	3,273
Total foodstuffs sold	3,799	3,857	4,067	4,283	4,441	4,469	4,651	4,830	4,858	4,996	5,071	2,508	2,183
Of which: social food items[1]	1,036	1,007	1,033	1,074	1,115	1,113	1,172	1,225	1,154	1,148	1,185	594	517
Total industrial goods sold	1,895	1,988	2,058	2,141	2,144	2,081	2,302	2,342	2,347	2,540	2,507	1,247	1,090
Stock of goods (end of year)	2,351	2,347	2,455	2,286	2,156	2,187	2,142	2,088	1,988	2,176	1,950	1,950	1,380
Excess demand registered at retail stores[2]	530	650	782	825	938	1,120	936	1,045	1,310	1,120	1,200	—	—
Profits of internal trading enterprises	168	185	168	167	172	168	161	152	139	139	91	57	48
							(Share of total circulation of goods)						
Total circulation of goods	100.0	100.0	100.0	100.0	100.0	100.0	100.0	100.0	100.0	100.0	100.0	—	—
Circulation of goods by cooperatives	13.4	13.5	14.1	14.0	14.1	14.7	14.0	13.7	13.9	14.1	12.8	—	—
Goods sold by internal trading enterprises	86.6	86.5	85.9	86.0	85.9	85.3	86.0	86.3	86.1	85.9	87.2	—	—
Total foodstuffs sold	57.8	57.0	57.0	57.3	57.9	58.2	57.6	58.1	58.0	57.0	58.3	—	—
Of which: social food items[1]	15.8	14.9	14.5	14.4	14.5	14.5	14.5	14.7	13.8	13.1	13.6	—	—
Total industrial goods sold	28.8	29.4	28.9	28.6	28.0	27.1	28.4	28.2	28.0	29.0	28.8	—	—
							(Percentage change over previous year)						
Total circulation of goods		2.8	5.5	4.8	2.6	0.2	5.4	2.7	0.7	4.7	-0.8	—	—
Circulation of goods by cooperatives		3.7	10.0	4.2	3.0	4.4	0.4	0.8	2.2	5.5	-9.4	—	—
Goods sold by internal trading enterprises		2.7	4.8	4.9	2.5	-0.5	6.3	3.0	0.5	4.6	0.6	—	—
Total foodstuffs sold		1.5	5.4	5.3	3.7	0.6	4.3	3.6	0.6	2.8	1.5	—	—
Of which: social food items[1]		-2.8	2.6	4.0	3.8	-0.2	5.3	4.5	-5.8	-0.5	3.2	—	—
Total industrial goods sold		4.9	3.5	4.0	0.1	-2.9	10.6	1.7	0.2	8.2	-1.3	—	—
Stock of goods (end of year)		-0.2	4.6	-6.9	-5.7	1.4	-2.1	-2.5	-4.8	9.5	-10.4	—	-29.2
Excess demand registered at retail stores[2]		22.6	20.3	5.5	13.7	19.4	-16.4	11.6	25.4	-14.5	7.1	—	—
Profits of internal trading enterprises		10.1	-9.2	-0.6	3.0	-2.3	-4.2	-5.6	-8.6	—	-34.5	—	-15.8

Sources: Ministry of Internal Trade; and State Planning Commission.

[1] Social food items are those items sold to the social sector, i.e., hospitals, schools, and military institutions.

[2] Excess demand registered at retail stores is the value of all commodities in current prices that were demanded by consumers at retail stores but were not available during the year.

Factor Markets: Organization and Development

Capital Stock and Investment

Albania's capital stock and capital formation process reflects a singular experience for a growing economy. As in many other planned economies, the objective of high growth via rapid industrialization was pursued vigorously, and, since the beginning of the planning period in 1951 and for 25 years, it was achieved through foreign aid. However, the severing of most foreign economic relations in the mid-1970s severely hampered growth. In particular, resources for new investment and capital replacement became more scarce over time, while the limited access to imported capital goods and the negligible technological innovation adversely affected the quality of the existing capital stock. Today, the capital stock across all sectors is largely obsolete. Rapid widespread replacements are required to prevent the complete collapse of production.

Nearly all investments, except for private housing in the cooperative sector, have been centrally planned and tightly controlled since 1950. Investment decisions were typically passed down through the state hierarchy. Since the early 1970s, enterprises have been allowed to initiate discussions on investment plans and output targets and each ministry had some discretion in deciding which projects to finance; final approval, however, was required from the Council of Ministers. Investment decisions on large projects and in critical sectors (such as mining) continued to be fully vested in the Council of Ministers.

In Albania, as in other centrally planned economies, investment rates were high and oriented toward heavy industry and construction activity. By the 1980s, however, a distinct declining trend in investment growth rates took place, reflecting high growth in consumption relative to output and lack of foreign capital inflows. Total net investment declined by an annual average rate of 0.8 percent a year during 1980–85 and by 2.4 percent in 1985–90. In 1990 alone, the decline in net capital formation was over 30 percent, reflecting acute shortages of domestic resources in a year of poor output performance and the depletion of foreign reserves available for importing capital (see Table 4).

Investment growth rates were also characterized by large annual fluctuations during 1980–90, reflecting bulk investments in some sectors in certain years. Although the average ratio of net fixed investment to NMP—24 percent—for 1980–90 continued to be impressive by international standards, the impact of capital formation on output was minimal.

Sectoral investment shares continued to reflect the emphasis given to the material sphere and industry. Gross fixed investment in the material sphere accounted for nearly 83 percent of total investments (Table A8). The share of the industrial (including mining) sector in the material sphere averaged 53 percent, while agriculture's share was 30 percent and transport's 6 percent.

Comparison of Capital Productivity with Other East European Countries

One way of measuring the impact of investment on output is to observe the trends in the incremental capital/output ratio using real net fixed capital formation as a proxy for investment. The inverse of this ratio is an indicator of the productivity of capital. Average capital productivity during 1981–90 was virtually nonexistent (0.04).

When Albania's performance in the 1980s is compared with some other East European countries such as Bulgaria and Czechoslovakia, a discouraging picture emerges (Table 12).[10] Bulgaria's average annual output growth during 1981–89 was much higher despite substantially lower real investment rates, because its capital productivity was twice as high as Albania's during the same period. Albania recorded an annual average output growth rate that was marginally higher than Czechoslovakia's during 1981–89; however, Albania needed to invest, on average, almost 10 percent more of its NMP than Czechoslovakia each year to compensate for lower productivity. In comparison with Romania during 1986–89 (the years for which data were available), Albania performed better in terms of both real NMP growth and productivity of capital.

Low capital productivity in Albania during the 1980s is not surprising; because investment funds were generally allocated according to planned priorities, they were not dependent on the economic viability of the investment project. More important, there was virtually no access to new foreign technology after 1978.

State of Capital Stock and Causes of Low Productivity

Capital stock across all sectors is virtually depleted and massive replacement and modernization is required. In view of the high capital intensity of

---

[10]Since data for 1990 are not available for some countries, averages for 1981–89 are compared.

Table 12. Comparison of Productivity of Capital with Other East European Countries, 1981–89

	1981	1982	1983	1984	1985	1986	1987	1988	1989	Average 1981–89[1]
Albania (Base year = 1986)										
Growth of real NMP	6.0	2.7	0.5	−2.9	1.8	6.2	−2.2	−0.5	11.7	2.5
Real net fixed investment ratio[2]	24.4	21.1	24.6	25.0	25.8	21.8	21.9	23.5	24.4	23.6
Productivity of capital[3,4]	0.25	0.13	0.02	−0.12	0.07	0.28	−0.10	−0.02	0.48	0.11
Bulgaria (Base year = 1982)										
Growth of real NMP	5.0	4.2	3.0	4.6	1.8	5.3	4.7	2.4	−1.51	3.4
Real net fixed investment ratio[2]	14.9	14.3	17.2	15.4	12.6	12.0	10.7	17.9	10.1	13.9
Productivity of capital[3,4]	0.34	0.29	0.17	0.30	0.14	0.44	0.44	0.13	−0.15	0.23
Czechoslovakia (Base year = 1984)										
Growth of real NMP	−0.1	0.2	2.3	3.5	3.0	2.6	2.1	2.3	0.7	1.8
Real net fixed investment ratio[2,5]	15.4	18.2	13.8	12.4	12.7	14.1	14.4	12.0	12.1	13.9
Productivity of capital[3,4]	−0.01	0.01	0.16	0.28	0.23	0.18	0.14	0.20	0.06	0.14
Romania (Base year = 1990)										
Growth of real NMP	. . .	. . .	. . .	. . .	. . .	3.0	0.7	−2.0	−7.9	−1.6
Real net fixed investment ratio[2]	. . .	. . .	. . .	. . .	. . .	24.1	24.1	22.1	20.2	22.6
Productivity of capital[3,4]	. . .	. . .	. . .	. . .	. . .	0.12	0.03	−0.09	−0.39	−0.08

Sources: Albania, State Planning Commission; IMF staff estimates for Romania and Yugoslavia; data from authorities in Bulgaria and Czechoslovakia.
[1] Averages for Romania are for 1986–89.
[2] Previous year's ratio. That is, $NI(t-1)/Y(t-1)$, where NI is net fixed investment, Y is net material product, and t is the current year.
[3] The productivity is given by $(Y(t) - Y(t-1))/NI(t-1)$.
[4] Inverse of incremental capital/output ratio.
[5] Since data on net investment in constant prices were not available, the implicit deflators of gross investment were used.

a substantial part of the industrial sector—particularly mining and energy—the resources required for replacement are enormous. Moreover, as local technology is outmoded, the need for foreign imports and external joint ventures is crucial.

The reasons for the obsolescence and low productivity may be directly traced to Albania's foreign economic policies over the last four decades. First, on account of its restrictive trade and exchange rate policies, Albania has faced foreign exchange shortages, a factor that has hampered imports from industrial countries. Second, almost all of Albania's capital goods imports originated from socialist countries, which frequently incorporated technologies that were inferior by industrial country standards. A number of investments were made in plant and equipment that was already outdated at the time of purchase. Attempts in recent years to upgrade equipment were often only halfhearted. Only key portions of a production process were modernized, sometimes with quite

advanced equipment from European sources, but such modernization did not have as much impact as it might because it was surrounded both upstream and downstream by inferior technology. Also, purchases of new capital equipment were generally not combined with agreements to upgrade technology.

Efforts were sometimes made to adapt and modify imported technology locally but these efforts do not appear to have been successful on account of inferior base technology and the limited ability of an isolated small country to foster innovation. The substitution of domestic for imported parts frequently resulted in the downgrading of machinery.

Equipment was maintained in service well beyond its normal economic life. Essentially, enterprises were allocated just enough resources—domestic and foreign—to keep the machinery running, but not to allow for adequate replacement and modernization. As a result, relatively significant amounts of domestic and foreign exchange resources were committed to repairing machines that would in normal circumstances have been scrapped.

Finally, a substantial proportion of industrial investment was expended with virtually no return. This investment is particularly obvious in the oil and gas sector, which absorbed roughly 40 percent of the investments carried out by the Ministry of Mines, Heavy Industry and Energy during the last decade, without discovering any substantial additional oil reserves.

Labor Market

Structure of Population, Labor Force, and Employment

During the last 15 years, Albania has experienced one of the highest rates of demographic growth among European countries. The sustained rise in population (3.3 million in 1990, up from 2.4 million in 1975; Table 13) reflected a deliberate demographic policy aimed at maintaining high and stable population growth rates, which averaged 2.2 percent a year in 1975–80 and 2 percent in 1980–90. Under this policy, social assistance programs provided grants to families for every child born, and extended paid maternity leave for pregnant working women and earlier retirement for mothers of large families. No family planning program has so far been implemented.[11] As a result of the rapid demographic growth, the average age of the population is about 27 years.

Working age starts at 15, and retirement is generally granted at the age of 60 for men and 55 for women. Population of working age grew at a much faster rate than total population—although its average annual growth rate declined from 3.1 percent in the second half of the 1970s to 2.2 percent in the second half of the 1980s—and its share rose from 52 percent in 1975 to 57 percent in 1990.[12]

The civilian labor force, estimated in the Albanian statistics by subtracting from the total population of working age the people considered inactive (such as students and disabled) and military personnel, rose at an average rate of 3.2 percent a year over the period 1975–90. The participation rate (in relation to population of working age) increased from 80 percent in 1980 to 83 percent in 1990. The share of women in the total labor force remained stable at about 48 percent.

In 1990, total registered employment in state enterprises, state farms, and cooperatives reached 1.4 million people (44 percent of total population). About two thirds of workers are employed in the state sector and the rest in the cooperative sector. No private sector employment was recorded during the 1980s. Over the decade, the structure of employment by sector of activity recorded only modest changes, as the shares of agriculture and construction declined slightly, to 49 percent and 7 percent, respectively, while the share of industry rose moderately (to 22.6 percent by 1990).

The right to work guaranteed by the 1976 Constitution and the rapid growth of the labor force required continuous government efforts to create jobs, irrespective of overall economic performance, and the absorption of increasing manpower occurred at the cost of productive efficiency. Over the period 1980–90, employment grew at an average annual rate (2.5 percent) that was equivalent to about three times the rate of growth of GDP at constant prices. The corresponding cumulative decline of labor productivity of about 15 percent over the decade reflected also the increasingly obsolete capital stock endowment per worker and the inadequate technological progress.[13] Many enterprises experienced excess or redundant manpower, which official estimates for 1990 put at over 14 percent of total employment. More recently, excess employment has become more acute, as thousands of workers on the payrolls of state enterprises have not actively contributed to production.[14]

Organization and Unemployment

The monitoring of labor market developments is organized at the local district level. In each of the

---

[11]As of 1989, some 55.2 percent of Albanian families were composed of 4–6 members, and 16 percent of 7–10 members. The latter proportion increases to 24 percent for families in rural areas, where about 64 percent of the population resides.

[12]The dependency ratio, measured in terms of total population (excluding recipients of pension income) declined from 2.57 in 1975 (each employed person maintains on average 1.57 additional people) to 2.05 in 1990. Recipients of pension income for old-age, invalidism, and social assistance (for orphans and relatives of war victims) increased from 110.2 thousand (4.6 percent of total population) in 1975 to 321.0 thousand (9.9 percent of total population) in 1990.

[13]An acceleration in the trend decline of labor productivity was evident. Between 1980 and 1986, real GDP increased on average by 2.6 percent a year and total employment by 3 percent, and in 1986–90, registered employment continued to increase (at an annual average rate of 1.7 percent) in spite of the real GDP decline (also at an annual average of 1.7 percent).

[14]The number of inactive workers is likely to have further increased by June 1991 as production in various sectors virtually stopped owing to shortages of intermediate inputs. According to current labor market regulations, inactive workers are entitled to 80 percent of their wages for an indefinite period.

Table 13. Population, Labor Force, and Employment, 1975–90
(In thousands: annual averages)

	1975	1980	1981	1982	1983	1984	1985	1986	1987	1988	1989	1990
Total population	2,400.8	2,670.5	2,723.7	2,781.4	2,838.1	2,896.7	2,957.4	3,016.2	3,076.1	3,138.1	3,199.2	3,255.9
Male	1,239.6	1,378.0	1,405.4	1,434.6	1,464.5	1,494.7	1,526.0	1,556.3	1,584.2	1,616.1	1,646.3	1,674.3
Female	1,161.2	1,292.5	1,318.3	1,346.8	1,373.6	1,402.0	1,431.4	1,459.9	1,491.9	1,522.9	1,552.9	1,581.6
Nonworking age population	1,139.8	1,199.8	1,210.1	1,228.8	1,239.7	1,250.7	1,269.3	1,286.9	1,309.6	1,328.2	1,355.9	1,375.2
Male	561.5	588.4	593.1	602.5	607.8	612.8	6'8.0	625.6	635.3	644.8	661.8	671.4
Female	578.3	611.4	617.0	626.3	631.9	637.9	651.3	661.3	674.3	683.4	694.1	703.8
Working age population[1]	1,261.0	1,470.7	1,513.6	1,552.6	1,598.4	1,646.0	1,688.1	1,729.3	1,766.5	1,809.9	1,843.3	1,880.7
Male	678.1	789.6	812.3	832.1	856.7	881.9	938.0	930.7	948.9	971.3	984.5	1,002.9
Female	582.9	681.1	701.3	720.5	741.7	764.1	780.1	798.6	817.6	838.6	858.8	877.8
Inactive and dependent population[2]	287.4	289.3	301.4	301.4	303.2	308.0	309.4	311.3	310.3	314.7	309.2	314.0
Male	…	171.8	179.2	178.3	179.5	182.0	186.1	190.2	191.0	193.4	186.4	189.0
Female	…	117.5	122.2	123.1	123.7	126.0	123.3	121.1	119.3	121.3	122.8	125.0
Labor force	973.5	1,181.4	1,212.2	1,251.2	1,295.2	1,338.0	1,378.7	1,418.0	1,456.2	1,495.2	1,534.1	1,566.7
Male	…	617.8	633.1	653.8	677.2	699.9	721.9	740.5	757.9	777.9	798.1	813.9
Female	…	563.6	579.1	597.4	618.0	638.1	656.8	677.5	698.3	717.3	736.0	752.8
Total employment	893.0	1,122.0	1,161.0	1,216.0	1,252.0	1,279.0	1,298.0	1,341.0	1,381.0	1,405.0	1,431.0	1,434.2
In state sector	503.0	655.0	676.0	709.0	735.0	757.0	769.0	800.0	830.0	852.0	881.0	906.3
In cooperative sector	390.0	467.0	485.0	507.0	517.0	522.0	529.0	541.0	551.0	553.0	550.0	527.9
Total unemployment	80.5	59.4	51.2	35.2	43.2	59.0	80.7	77.0	75.2	90.2	103.1	132.5
Registered unemployment[3]	16.5	19.5	21.5	17.4	21.2	25.5	30.9	37.1	30.3	30.3	28.7	33.2
Male[3]	3.0	4.8	5.6	5.0	5.8	7.1	10.4	12.9	10.4	10.1	10.9	13.6
Female[3]	13.5	14.7	15.9	12.4	15.4	18.4	20.5	24.2	19.9	20.2	17.8	19.6
Memorandum item:												
Labor force[3]	984.0	1,193.1	1,231.3	1,272.9	1,317.6	1,358.5	1,399.0	1,437.0	1,475.4	1,514.8	1,553.4	1,582.0
Male[3]	…	623.9	642.3	665.4	689.0	710.9	732.9	748.0	767.9	787.8	808.4	820.5
Female[3]	…	569.2	589.0	607.5	628.6	647.6	666.1	689.0	707.5	727.0	745.0	761.5

Source: Statistical Directorate and Employment Directorate, State Planning Commission.
[1]Working age is from 15–59 years for men, and from 15–54 years for women.
[2]Includes disabled, students, and military forces.
[3]End of period data.

Chart 10. Assets and Liabilities of Households, 1980–90
(In percent of GDP)

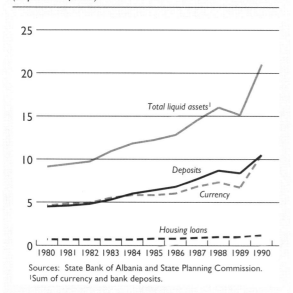

Sources: State Bank of Albania and State Planning Commission.
[1]Sum of currency and bank deposits.

26 districts a labor office is attached to the local government executive committee. State farms and enterprises specify to the local labor office their demand for labor in terms of workers' qualifications, and the labor office independently selects and appoints the appropriate candidates.

Labor mobility has in the past been severely impeded by administrative regulations on mobility of the population. Mobility from rural to urban areas required permission from both village and urban authorities, which was granted only if the central plan indicated emerging labor shortages in specific areas, or if someone was moving to join the internal security forces. Mobility between enterprises was also discouraged, since changing a job assignment was considered undesirable. Some of these barriers to labor and population mobility have been formally removed by the 1990 reforms, but in practice labor mobility continues to be effectively limited by severe housing shortages.

Over the 1980s, the inability of the economy to absorb the rapid increase in the labor force revealed itself in declining productivity, disguised unemployment, but also in an increase in open unemployment[15] (Chart 7), which in the Albanian

definition is residually derived by subtracting the number of registered employed from the total labor force. After fluctuating around an average of 4.4 percent in 1980–86, the unemployment rate increased from 5.2 percent in 1987 to 8.5 percent in 1990.[16]

In the Albanian definition, total unemployment greatly exceeds the number of unemployed registered at labor offices as actively looking for a job. Nearly half of the unregistered unemployment in rural areas refers to women not actively searching for a job because of their large family, with the remainder accounted for by discouraged working-age population. Unemployment registration was in fact limited by the widespread dislike of working conditions in state farms and enterprises, which provided most job vacancies administered through the local labor offices,[17] and by the lack of unemployment benefits, which reduced financial incentives for the unemployed to register.[18]

Wages

Wage Determination System

The system of wage determination has been in effect since 1967, with relatively minor reforms introduced in 1990. Until 1990, wage setting was centralized (except in the cooperatives, where wages were output determined), with pay levels fixed by law for five-year periods at the beginning of each plan, and with little change from one plan to the next. Wages were supposedly set with reference to the level of output, labor productivity, and the basic consumption needs of the population, as reflected in minimum cost of living estimates. Wage indexation existed to the extent that cost of living considerations influenced minimum wage setting. All wages were paid in cash.

Wage policy has been inspired by the broad principle of narrowing the remuneration gap be-

---

[15]The deteriorating employment prospects and standards of living caused waves of emigration from Albania in 1990–91. Official estimates gave the number as over 7,000 between July and December 1990. During the first quarter of 1991, emigration was estimated to have increased to some 30,000.

The exodus to Italy that took place in March 1991 was quantified at about 25,000, of which about 2,000–3,000 later returned to Albania; in August 1991, another 18,000 people attempted to emigrate.

[16]In 1990, total unemployment averaged about 133,000 people, and increased to 140,000–150,000 by yearend. About 48 percent of unemployed were between 15 and 24 years of age, 29 percent between 25 and 35, and 22 percent were over 36 years of age.

[17]The rapid increase in unemployment not officially registered in 1990 was in part associated with expectations of a land reform that would increase the number and size of private agricultural plots, and thus provide an alternative to state sector employment.

[18]At end-April 1991, the Parliament approved a law introducing social assistance for the unemployed, but the program is still not operative.

tween physical and intellectual work, between sectors (agriculture and industry in particular), and between workers with different qualifications. By law, wage differentiation was confined within a ratio of 1 to 2 between the average wage of all blue-collar workers in the economy and the highest wage of managers. Differences in wages were regulated both across sectors (to remunerate physically difficult working conditions specific to the sector, and the perceived relative importance of the sector), and within each sector (to remunerate higher responsibilities).[19] Salaries of managers and technical employees were also to some extent differentiated, with remuneration of enterprise directors exceeding salaries of the least qualified white-collar workers in the same branch by a margin of about 40 percent, and varying according to performance and size of production units.

Bonuses and penalties linking remuneration to achievement of plan targets were first introduced in 1980, with an asymmetric scheme limited to a range of 5 percent of remuneration for bonuses and 10 percent for penalties. In 1985, special bonuses associated with overfulfillment of plan targets were used in several branches (chromium and oil industry, agriculture, exporting sectors, etc.), together with penalties only for managers (up to 10 percent of the annual salary) if the enterprise's performance fell short of predetermined levels. In 1990, penalties for unrealized planned profits were set at up to 10 percent of both wages of workers and salaries of managers; bonuses to both workers and managers involved the distribution of up to 50 percent of profits above planned levels, up to a limit of three months of wages and salaries.[20]

Wage Developments and Relativities

Average effective earnings (including bonuses and penalties related to the achievement of plan targets as well as partial wage payments during work interruptions) have changed relatively little in nominal terms over the last 15 years (Table 14, Chart 8). For the total economy, they were in 1990 only 3 percent above the level in 1975, in-creased in nominal terms by an average annual rate of 0.8 percent. In terms of the official retail price index, real average effective earnings for the whole economy rose over the decade by 10.7 percent, or by an annual average of 1 percent. In terms of GDP deflator, real effective earnings rose by 14.1 percent, compared with a decline in average productivity of 14.7 percent.[21]

During 1980–90, average effective earnings per unit of output (not including all labor costs, as they exclude time-varying state enterprise contributions for the financing of social security) rose by 28 percent.[22] About two thirds of this increase are due to the marked decline in labor productivity over the decade. Therefore, despite the low growth of nominal wages, the loss of productive efficiency associated with the pressure to absorb the increasing labor force translated into a marked reduction in cost effectiveness.

Relative wages did not show important changes over the 1980s. State sector earnings fluctuated at about 21 percent above, and cooperative sector earnings at about 32 percent below, the national average. Wages in industry, transport and communications, trade and catering, and in the services of the nonmaterial sphere declined in relation to the national average, while wages in agriculture, construction, and other material sphere sectors increased. In 1990 relative wages varied between a lower bound given by remuneration in agriculture and trade, and an upper bound for earnings in the central government sector.[23]

In theory, minimum wages were set by taking into account the minimum cost of living, but in practice a large portion of the working population received wages below the estimated minimum cost of living, computed for the first time in 1975 and re-estimated in 1988 (both set at leks 450 a month). On the basis of the 1988 review, in September 1990 the minimum monthly wage (for many years set at leks 350 a month) was increased to leks 450 to match the minimum cost of living, affecting the incomes of some 27 percent of workers previously paid less. Together with the adjustment in the minimum wage level, additional wage increases (mostly concentrated at the lower

---

[19]The wage spectrum across sectors is limited. Within sectors, the highest ratio between maximum and minimum wage rates was reduced to 1.45 in coal mining after September 1990, while the lowest ratio has always applied to commercial trade (with pay variation limited as of May 1991 within a 9 percent range).

[20]These partial wage reforms remained conditional on the achievement of plan targets. In conditions characterized by scarcity of raw materials and obsolete capital endowment, penalties may have exercised downward pressure on wages and salaries.

[21]Some caution is required in interpreting developments in labor productivity, since employment figures overestimate the effective utilization of the labor factor in production.

[22]Preliminary estimates obtained by increasing average effective earnings by social security contribution rates paid by state enterprises point to an increase in labor costs per unit of output during 1980–90 equal to 30 percent, equivalent on average to 2.7 percent a year.

[23]In 1990, wages in the industrial sector were on aggregate about 13 percent above the national average. However, within the sector, wages in mining were substantially higher.

Table 14. Average Monthly Earnings, 1975-90
(Actual, including bonuses and penalties, in leks)

	1975	1980	1981	1982	1983	1984	1985	1986	1987	1988	1989	1990
Total socialist sector	447	420	431	448	449	442	446	451	443	445	466	459
State sector	536	534	530	536	536	536	535	540	542	545	550	561
Cooperatives sector[1]	331	259	293	323	326	305	315	318	293	291	330	284
Material sphere	430	391	405	424	425	416	421	426	417	418	440	437
Agriculture[1]	...	319	343	376	377	364	369	371	354	353	380	376
Industry	...	517	508	511	510	501	508	514	516	517	527	521
Transport and communications	...	568	534	547	554	547	541	553	537	540	536	519
Trade and catering	...	450	443	446	439	447	434	440	448	445	455	457
Construction	...	443	462	443	447	457	462	492	510	523	544	540
Other	...	481	470	483	483	485	486	486	469	513	634	668
Nonmaterial sphere	553	570	569	570	573	573	574	577	579	582	590	591
Education	...	591	589	592	590	598	602	607	609	617	622	623
Health	...	491	491	502	498	500	510	514	515	516	520	523
Public services (transport, trade)	...	549	544	530	550	529	518	528	550	540	533	540
Scientific research institutions	...	...	...	...	...	...	...	601	589	610	611	612
Central Government	...	...	...	...	...	...	...	876	937	937	935	937
Specialized organizations[2]	...	...	...	...	...	...	...	768	746	768	776	778
Other	...	649	651	657	653	660	659	615	587	629	633	631

Source: Statistical Directorate and Wage Directorate, State Planning Commission.
[1] Excluding remuneration in kind for self-consumption.
[2] Social and political organizations.

Chart 8. Average Monthly Earnings,[1] 1980–90

(In leks)

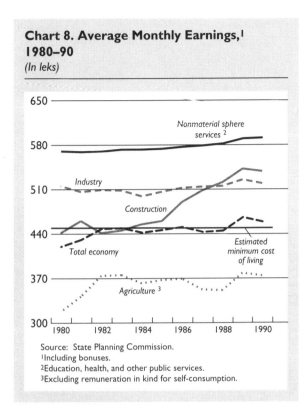

Source: State Planning Commission.
[1]Including bonuses.
[2]Education, health, and other public services.
[3]Excluding remuneration in kind for self-consumption.

end of the pay range) occurred in September 1990. Despite these increases, average effective earnings declined in 1990 as workers received only partial payments during the frequent work interruptions caused by power failures and insufficient raw materials.

Social Security

The social security system provides for old-age pensions, social assistance pensions for orphans and relatives of war victims, pensions for invalids, and maternity benefits. In 1989, 79 percent of social security expenditures were allocated to pensions,[24] 10 percent to temporary disability benefits, and 8.5 percent to maternity benefits. Social security benefits are financed by state enterprise contributions, with a rate that increased from 11 percent of wages in 1975–79 to 21 percent in January 1991. (The social security contribution rate was equal to 13 percent in 1980–85 and 15 percent in 1986–90.)

---

[24]According to the State Planning Commission, in 1980–89 social security expenditures for pensions increased at an average annual rate of 7.9 percent. The number of recipients of pension incomes rose in the same period at an average annual rate of 6.8 percent.

Old-age pensions are generally granted at the age of 60 for men and 55 for women. Under present arrangements, normal pensions correspond to 70 percent of the former wage. Recently, early retirement became available with pensions corresponding to 60 percent of the former wage.

Price Determination

Price System

Albania was for a long time a fixed-price economy. The Council of Ministers established retail prices for the main commodities and set guidelines for the other state institutions that deal with prices. The Ministry of Finance was mainly responsible for establishing prices at the wholesale level, prices of public services, and prices of imported goods allocated through the plan.

Prices of imported raw materials were fixed at the beginning of each plan for the five-year period, taking into account international prices and the "economic exchange rate." The domestic (wholesale) prices of local raw materials and of exportables did not change as a result of variations in international prices. Any difference between fixed domestic wholesale prices and international prices was absorbed by the state budget. For imported capital goods and equipment, international price variations within the five-year planning period were transmitted to domestic costs of production only through changes in amortization rates over a number of years, with practically no impact on prices. This system ensured the virtually complete insulation of Albanian domestic prices from international price fluctuations.

For domestic prices, three categories were of particular importance: wholesale prices; retail prices; and agricultural prices. When prices in all of these categories were fixed below production or acquisition costs, the resulting losses of producing or trading enterprises were covered by the state budget.

Wholesale prices were determined by the Ministry of Finance, and applied to transactions between state enterprises for raw materials, intermediate goods, and domestically produced machinery. At the beginning of the planning process, enterprises submitted a cost analysis supporting the formulation of a tentative wholesale price proposal. Once the plan was approved, a set of prices was specified and remained fixed for five years. In setting wholesale prices, a profit margin was added to the cost of production that included transportation expenses, and no turnover tax was added. Wholesale prices did not reflect fluctua-

Table 15. Wholesale and Retail Price Indices, 1975–90
(1986 = 100)

	1975	1980	1981	1982	1983	1984	1985	1986	1987	1988	1989	1990
Wholesale prices												
Industry	108.2	108.2	105.0	105.0	105.0	105.0	105.0	100.0	100.0	100.0	100.0	100.0
Construction	108.9	108.9	106.1	106.1	106.1	106.1	106.1	100.0	100.0	100.0	100.0	100.0
Agriculture	98.7	98.7	96.8	96.8	96.8	96.8	96.8	100.0	100.0	100.0	100.0	100.0
Retail prices	101.3	101.3	100.7	100.0	100.0	100.0	100.0	100.0	100.0	100.0	100.0	100.0

Source: Statistical Directorate, State Planning Commission.

tions in the international price of imported machinery and equipment, as the impact on production costs through amortization was generally absorbed by enterprise profits, and indirectly by the budget through reduced net surplus transfers. Only rarely, when changes in import prices were too large to be absorbed by the enterprises' profits, was the wholesale price allowed to change.

Retail prices remained fixed for many years, and were determined as the sum of wholesale prices, a turnover tax, and a margin of intermediation for the internal trade enterprises. The producing enterprise sold its products to the internal trade organization at a price including the turnover tax, and the final buyer was charged the retail price inclusive of a margin of commercial intermediation. In the rare cases of wholesale price variation within the plan period, the turnover tax was adjusted to maintain the fixed retail price and the margin of intermediation.

Agricultural prices involved a system of procurement prices paid to producers and fixed by the Council of Ministers. For agricultural products other than fruit and vegetables, procurement prices differed according to whether farming took place in lowland, hills, or mountain land, irrespective of whether they were produced by state farms or cooperatives. The state budget subsidized agricultural production on hills and mountains through setting relatively higher prices, especially for unprofitable production in mountainous areas. These agricultural products were distributed through *grumbullims*. The *grumbullim* purchased all the agricultural commodities from the producers at procurement prices, and sold to (1) enterprises using these products as raw materials, at a wholesale price set as the sum of procurement price plus an intermediation margin for the *grumbullim*; or (2) internal trade enterprises, at a sale price that

was equal to the retail price minus the margin of intermediation of internal trade enterprises. If this sale price was lower than the procurement price, the *grumbullim* was subsidized by the budget. For fruit and vegetables, procurement prices were not subject to land classification criteria and were set every 15 days by the executive committees in the local districts within fixed maximum and minimum limits. For these products, seasonal and local price variation was therefore allowed.

Price Developments and Recent Reforms

Official aggregate indicators of price developments (Table 15) confirm the complete fixity of wholesale prices *within* the last two five-year planning periods.[25] In addition, they point to declining wholesale price indices for industry and construction (from one plan to the next), to a rising index for agriculture, and to the complete fixity of retail prices since 1982, with a marginal decline from 1980 to 1982.

In the course of 1990, some partial price reforms were introduced. In May 1990 industrial enterprises were encouraged to set autonomously the prices of new production for a number of nonessential commodities (such as glass and plastic products). In June–July 1990, price incentives were introduced in the agricultural sector for production above plan targets, with margins of 25–40 percent above normal procurement prices, which, as retail prices were kept constant, entailed increased budget subsidies. In addition, prices of fruit and vegetables were allowed to be determined by demand and supply, but within ceilings set by

---

[25]In spite of widespread shortages of goods, no organized unofficial markets emerged, and, according to the authorities, the development of illegal parallel markets has been kept at an insignificant level.

the Council of Ministers. In 1990, legal parallel markets for private plots' agricultural products were also allowed for the first time. The worsening inflationary pressures associated with the shortages of many essential commodities could then be revealed by the margins between official and private plots' prices, which for some products (such as meat and potatoes) rose from 33–75 percent to 100 percent between the last quarter of 1990 and February 1991. In March–April 1991, the price differential remained stable, and in some cases it declined in May–June 1991. In addition to better weather, a positive response to higher-than-official prices improved the supply of agricultural products sold in private markets, which increased rapidly following the spontaneous dismantling of agricultural cooperatives in the second quarter of 1991.

Macroeconomic Policies

As in other centrally planned systems, the primary role of macroeconomic policies was to ensure the achievement of the planned physical targets. Fiscal policy was used to mobilize resources and channel them to fulfill the quantitative plan, while monetary policy was largely passive and essentially was to accommodate the resource requirements. Interest rates played no role in allocating resources, and exchange rate policy was limited to determining the rates for accounting purposes, as domestic prices were insulated from changes in world prices through a system of taxes and subsidies.

Budgetary Organization and Fiscal Developments

Role of Fiscal Policy

Fiscal policy basically had four functions. First, the state budget served as the financial counterpart of the quantitative plan, and its primary function was to accommodate the plan targets. It also provided a mechanism for automatic financial correction of deviations from the planned targets, particularly in funding investment expenditures and enterprise losses, both planned and unplanned. Second, albeit to a limited extent, it provided financial control over quantitative planning to equate demand for and supply of available resources. Third, without capital markets and an active monetary policy, the budget was the principal instrument of resource allocation. Virtually all financial surpluses of enterprises were transferred

to, and all their costs financed by, the budget. And finally, until the late 1970s, it was instrumental in ensuring macroeconomic stability. The budget deficits until 1978 were on average relatively small, and were financed by large amounts of concessional foreign credit. The excess of the foreign inflows was sterilized by setting up a reserve account ("Reserve Fund") in the central bank. Since 1979, although the inflow of foreign resources ceased, the fiscal stance has not been adjusted, resulting in substantial imbalances after 1983.

Structure of Government

The Government consists of the Central Government and 26 local governments. The Central Government comprises the Council of Ministers and the branch ministries; local governments include the executive committees of each local district, which are under the jurisdiction of the Ministry of Finance. Before 1991, the public sector covered almost the whole economy, excluding households. In addition to the Central Government and the local governments, the public sector included the enterprise sector, agricultural state farms and cooperatives, and the financial institutions.

The state budget encompasses the national budget (covering the Central Government) and the budgets of the 26 local districts. The national budget includes all expenditures related to state enterprises and farms under the jurisdiction of branch ministries, expenditures on central administration, defense and security, telecommunications, and expenditures such as price subsidies and those on foreign trade operations. The local budgets comprise all expenditures related to enterprises under the local district's jurisdiction, excluding the above-mentioned subsidies and outlays on social security.

From the late 1940s until 1990, the relations between the Central Government and the local authorities remained virtually unchanged. All revenues represented resources of the Central Government, the sole body responsible for tax policy. For local districts where revenues were planned to exceed expenditures, the budget determined the share of revenue that could be retained. For those districts where the plan envisaged expenditures higher than revenues, the budget determined the amount of additional resources to be transferred to that region. Local governments could not initiate expenditure on their own, and were not allowed to use bank credit, or any other form of financing. On average, about 45 percent of the consolidated budget was executed at the local level.

Box 3. The Dual Budgetary System

From the early 1980s, what amounts to a dual budgetary system was introduced. Since the state budget was required by law to be in surplus, there existed, in practice, an official "surplus budget" and an unofficial "deficit budget"; the latter functioned to finance expenditures not covered by regular budgetary revenues. The unofficial budget was not made public, and if additional expenditures were committed during the year, these were discretely managed by the Ministry of Finance and the branch ministries.

The need to introduce a dual system in the early 1980s stemmed from the legal impact on state resources of the constitutional ban on foreign capital inflows in 1976. Prior to the ban, the legal requirement of a surplus budget was ensured by recording foreign credit, which had been substantial in the 1970s, as regular revenue. After the ban and the interruption of foreign assistance, the Government was able to comply with this legal requirement despite large expenditures by separating the past accumulation of foreign capital and by recording them in the "Reserve Fund," a special kind of government deposit at the central bank. The resources of the Reserve Fund were occasionally enhanced by selling the strategic commodity reserves of the Government and by confiscating enterprise deposits. The Reserve Fund functioned, in practice, as the "unofficial budget," to cover planned expenditures in the official budget that could not be financed owing to revenue shortfalls. In addition, the unofficial budget financed outlays that were planned but not formally budgeted, such as some types of enterprise investments, as well as expenditures that were neither planned nor budgeted, such as various forms of enterprise subsidies. Therefore, the Reserve Fund was, for all practical and analytical purposes, a parallel budget rather than a typical extrabudgetary fund, as it was not earmarked to finance specific budgetary outlays but those that could not be covered by regular revenues.

Budgetary Process

A distinctive characteristic of the budgetary system since the early 1980s has been the coexistence of a dual budgetary system, consisting of the official "surplus budget" and an unofficial "deficit budget" (see Box 3 for details). This distinction helped in running deficits when needed, since the official budget was required by law to be in surplus. The primary sources of revenue for the unofficial budget were foreign capital inflows (until 1978), sales from the strategic commodity reserves, and occasional confiscation of state enterprise deposits.

Budgetary preparation and procedures differed for the two budgets. The official budget was prepared by the Ministry of Finance, in collaboration with the branch ministries and the Planning Commission, and was approved by the Parliament. Because by law the official budget had to be in surplus, and at the same time provide for expenditure levels consistent with the quantitative plan targets, it typically contained unrealistically high revenue projections. When, as expected, revenue shortfalls emerged, uncovered outlays were shifted to the unofficial budget and financed by the Reserve Fund. Additional expenditures committed during the year were also financed by the Reserve Fund.

Budgetary procedures for the unofficial budget varied by type of expenditure. In addition to covering shortfalls in planned and budgeted expenditures (arising from shortfalls in planned revenues), this budget also financed outlays that were actually planned but not formally budgeted (for example, some types of enterprise investments), as well as expenditures that were neither planned nor budgeted (typically, various forms of enterprise subsidies). For some types of expenditures (such as enterprise subsidies), authorization was automatic; for others, it remained at the discretion of the Ministry of Finance and the State Planning Commission.

The consolidated—official and unofficial—budget was implemented at the national and the local levels. The official budget always closed on the last day of December, with a complementary period of 10–15 days, while no formal closing date was fixed for the unofficial budget (although it usually closed by the following May). The closing of the budgets, however, did not necessarily ensure the settling of all outstanding government obligations, which often remained unsettled and were carried over to the next fiscal year in the form of government arrears to the enterprise sector.

During the year, the Ministry of Finance compiled and reported only the official budget, while information on and monitoring of expenditures outside this budget remained sketchy and disorganized. Therefore, the authorities had neither the necessary information nor the mechanism to restrain expenditure in case of revenue shortfalls. Indeed, the separation of the two budgets reduced transparency in the fiscal accounts and contributed to the lack of budgetary control, particularly because deficits in the unofficial budget were financed automatically by drawing down deposits in the Reserve Fund.

In addition to the Reserve Fund, there were other smaller extrabudgetary funds and accounts.[26] The most important were the strategic commodity reserves (such as raw materials, petroleum, spare parts, foodstuffs, and other consumer goods), which were managed by some state enterprises, under the direct control of the Prime Minister. These reserves were replenished by annual budgetary allocations from the official budget to these enterprises and were used to alleviate supply constraints. They were also occasionally used to reduce the size of the fiscal deficit, by transferring the proceeds from reserve sales to the budget and recording them as nontax revenues.

Another extrabudgetary fund recorded the Government's reserves of precious metals, held with the central bank. Purchases of precious metals were also made from budgetary outlays, and the proceeds from sales recorded as nontax revenues. Other accounts held at the central bank included the account in foreign exchange of the Council of Ministers and the accounts of branch ministries originating from some earmarked reserves.

Fiscal Developments Until 1990[27]

During 1947–78, budgetary policies were typically geared toward maximizing growth through high levels of investment—nearly 30 percent of GDP.[28] Because national savings were insufficient to finance investments of this magnitude, foreign resources were used to close the domestic gap. Moreover, since household savings and investment were negligible, and budgetary intermediation in the enterprise sector was almost complete, developments in national savings and investment closely corresponded to those in government savings and investment.

The large fall in imported machinery and equipment after the cessation of foreign financing in 1978 induced a marked reduction of investment outlays. The favorable impact on the budget was reinforced by three developments that helped generate small fiscal surpluses in 1979–82. First, major investments carried out in the 1970s in heavy industry, particularly in the oil sector, started to

mature, and exports increased sharply. Second, export prices improved because of the 1979 second oil shock and the shift from bilateral nonconvertible trade agreements with China toward world markets, with a favorable effect on the budget through price-equating foreign trade taxes (increasing by a cumulative 6 percent of GDP in 1979–82). Finally, Albania's unilateral cancellation of its debt to China relieved the budget of heavy debt-service payments.

Fiscal imbalances emerged in 1983–85 (Table 16 and Table A11) on account of three factors—continued high levels of budgetary investment (averaging 28 percent of GDP a year); foreign trade losses reflected in the budget from the tax subsidy scheme that equated domestic to world prices; and increasing social security deficits (which reflected demographic factors as well as relatively low contribution rates), from 1 percent of GDP in 1980 to 2.2 percent in 1985. The resulting fiscal deficits (Chart 9), averaging 3.5 percent of GDP annually, were covered by drawing down Reserve Fund deposits.

The Five-Year Plan beginning in 1986 aimed at reducing domestic demand and strengthening export sector performance. Accordingly, fiscal policies were temporarily tightened through a reduction in expenditure (mainly enterprise investments and subsidies), from an annual average of 54 percent of GDP in 1983–85 to 50 percent in 1986–87 (Table 16). However, revenue declined during the same period, from an average of 50.5 percent of GDP to slightly below 49 percent, reflecting lower nontax revenue and a steep fall in profit transfers from the enterprises (from an average of 14.7 percent of GDP to 10.8 percent) (Table A12).[29] Social security contribution rates were increased from 13 percent to 15 percent, resulting in a social security deficit of less than 2 percent of GDP. Since expenditure cuts more than compensated for the decline in revenue, the fiscal deficit was reduced from an average of 3.5 percent in 1983–85 to an average of less than 1 percent in 1986–87.

Stabilization efforts proved to be only temporary, and tight fiscal policies were replaced by renewed expansion in 1988–89. However, in contrast to 1983–85, when high levels of investment were the main cause of fiscal imbalance, subsidies for foreign trade and enterprises were primary fac-

---

[26]All these accounts are included in the state budget estimates presented in this paper.

[27]The term budget here refers to the consolidated state budget, comprising both the official surplus budget and the unofficial deficit budget.

[28]Gross investment, as appears in the budget.

[29]This decline in turn resulted from the weakening in enterprise profitability caused by decreasing productivity, reflecting the obsolete capital stock, overmanning of enterprises to maintain full employment, and the Government's decision to reduce industrial wholesale prices in 1986, at the beginning of the Five-Year Plan.

Table 16. Fiscal Indicators, 1982–90
(In percent of GDP)

	1982	1983	1984	1985	1986	1987	1988	1989	1990
Total revenue	52.0	50.0	50.9	50.6	48.7	49.2	53.2	48.2	47.0
Tax revenue	44.7	43.4	45.2	45.6	45.0	46.2	45.3	44.2	43.7
Of which:									
Turnover tax	21.7	20.7	19.4	19.7	22.3	22.8	22.8	22.6	24.2
Transfers from enterprises									
(profit tax plus amortization)	18.9	18.1	21.0	21.2	17.2	17.8	16.8	16.1	13.1
Of which:									
Profit transfers[1]	. . .	. . .	14.8	14.6	10.8	10.8	10.3	10.6	7.8
Nontax revenue	7.3	6.6	5.7	5.0	3.7	3.0	7.9	4.0	3.3
Total expenditure	51.9	53.9	55.4	52.7	48.8	50.9	54.4	56.8	63.6
Current expenditure	23.9	25.3	25.3	26.2	23.7	25.5	27.9	27.6	38.6
Of which:									
Turnover tax									
Wage bill	6.4	6.5	6.8	6.7	6.8	7.0	7.2	6.6	8.0
Total subsidies	6.8	7.5	6.5	7.3	5.7	6.7	8.5	8.7	16.1
Of which:									
Enterprise	4.3	5.8	4.8	5.4	4.2	4.9	6.8	6.6	14.3
Consumer price	2.2	1.7	1.6	1.7	1.3	1.9	1.7	1.7	1.8
Social security	4.7	5.3	5.9	6.1	6.4	6.7	7.3	7.1	8.8
Total investment	28.0	27.9	29.7	26.2	25.5	25.7	26.4	29.3	25.9
Use of funds of Council of Ministers, branch ministries (−:increase in funds)	0.1	0.7	0.4	0.3	−0.5	−0.4	0.1	−0.2	−0.9
Fiscal balance, commitment basis	0.1	−3.9	−4.5	−2.1	−0.1	−1.7	−1.2	−8.6	−16.6
Fiscal balance, cash basis	0.1	−3.9	−2.3	−4.3	−0.1	−1.7	−0.2	−5.5	−4.8
Memorandum item:									
Fiscal balance, excluding the impact of the use of State Emergency Fund and confiscation of enterprise deposits	0.1	−3.9	−4.5	−2.1	−0.1	−1.7	−5.9	−9.5	−16.6

Sources: Data provided by the Albanian authorities; and IMF staff calculations.
[1]Until 1984, profit transfers were lumped together with amortization.

tors in 1988–89. Enterprise subsidies rose from an average of 4.5 percent of GDP in 1986–87 to 6.7 percent in 1988–89, reflecting the continued worsening of enterprise profitability.[30] Revenues, on the other hand, remained broadly unchanged in relation to GDP, as receipts from turnover taxes compensated for the decline in profit and amortization transfers. Meanwhile, social security outlays continued to outpace the increase in social security contributions, and the deficit on social security again exceeded 2 percent of GDP. Under these circumstances, to check the rate of monetary

---

[30]A small portion of this increase may have been attributable to the introduction of some cautious regulatory changes in 1988, which granted very limited financial autonomy to certain enterprises (for example, in heavy industry) but kept all prices unchanged.

expansion and to ease the shortages of certain commodities, the Government decided to draw on its commodity reserves, and to confiscate in 1988–89 about 15 percent of enterprise deposits. As a result, the fiscal deficit reached 1.2 and 8.6 percent of GDP, respectively, in 1988 and 1989. However, if these essentially nonrecurrent revenues were excluded from nontax revenues, the fiscal deficit would have been equivalent to 5.9 and 9.5 percent of GDP, respectively. The Government also began to incur arrears to the enterprise sector, amounting to 4.1 percent of GDP at the end of 1989. Accordingly, the fiscal deficit, on a cash basis, was only 0.2 percent and 5.5 percent of GDP, respectively, in 1988 and 1989 (Table 16).

Against the backdrop of a 13 percent decline in output in 1990, the fiscal deficit, on a commitment basis, rose sharply from leks 1.6 billion (8.6

Chart 9. Selected Fiscal Indicators, 1982–90
(In percent of GDP)

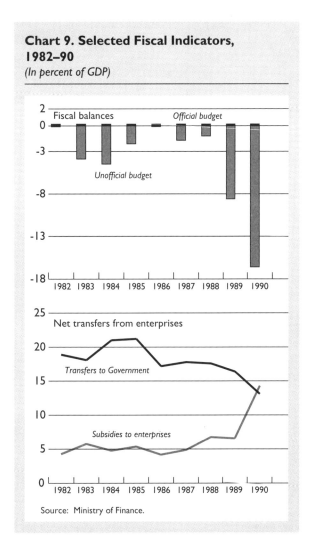

Source: Ministry of Finance.

an increase in social security outlays that resulted in a social security deficit equivalent to 3 percent of GDP.

Although the size of the fiscal imbalance in 1990 was related to the sharp contraction in economic activity, it also reflected lack of budgetary control. Moreover, after mid-1990, enterprise claims on the budget for subsidies on production losses could not be thoroughly scrutinized as substantial organizational changes affected the different branch ministries.

Unlike in the past, only a fraction of the fiscal deficit was monetized in 1990 (leks 773 million), and the bulk gave rise to a significant buildup of government arrears to the enterprise sector (leks 1.9 billion). By end-1990, the cumulative stock of these arrears reached leks 2.7 billion, or 16.5 percent of GDP.

Revenues

As in other centrally planned economies (CPEs), the primary goal of tax policy in Albania was to ensure central intervention in the economic decision-making process of productive units by siphoning off virtually all financial surpluses of state enterprises and state farms.

The budget relied on four major revenue sources (Table A12). Since the primary goal was to ensure the collection of the planned level of revenues, those taxes were favored that could (1) generate planned revenues with minimal error (such as taxes over which the enterprises have the least leeway to "bargain" once set); (2) provide the best information on implementing the quantitative plan; and (3) be easily monitored and collected. Therefore, the turnover tax became (as in other CPEs) the dominant source of revenue. It averaged about 45 percent and 52 percent of total tax revenue during 1981–85 and 1986–90, respectively. Enterprise taxes in the form of profit and amortization transfers accounted for about 36 percent of total revenue during 1986–90, declining from an average of 44 percent during 1981–85. The share of social security contributions gradually increased from about 8 percent in 1982 to roughly 14 percent in 1990. The share of nontax revenue was lower, accounting for an average of 10 percent of total revenue between 1981 and 1990. Nontax revenue was composed mainly of income from budgetary institutions (fees from nurseries, schools, theaters, movies, etc.), revenue from government services to the agricultural sector, the confiscation of enterprise deposits, and the use of proceeds from sales of strategic commodity reserves.

percent of GDP) in 1989 to leks 2.7 billion (16.6 percent of GDP) in 1990. In relation to GDP, revenues declined marginally, by 15.3 percent in nominal terms in 1990. In nominal terms, the profit transfers declined by 35.7 percent and amortization transfers by 17.8 percent. Turnover taxes declined by 6.8 percent, reflecting a drop in consumption of certain heavily taxed items, such as clothing. In contrast, total expenditure rose from 56.8 percent of GDP in 1989 to 63.6 percent of GDP in 1990, although in nominal terms expenditure declined by merely 2.6 percent (Tables A12 and A13). While outlays for investment contracted by 23 percent, albeit from an exceptionally high level in 1989, current expenditure increased by 21.5 percent, fueled by an 87 percent increase in subsidies for enterprise losses, a 4.5 percent rise in wages despite the sharp fall in production, and

Table 17. General Government Tax Revenue in CPEs, 1986
(In percent of GDP)

	Albania	Bulgaria	Czechoslovakia	Romania
Total	45.0	49.6	48.6	39.0
Profit taxes and transfers[1]	18.0[2]	18.7	25.1	. . .
Income taxes	—	4.0	5.0	. . .
Turnover taxes	22.3	16.5	15.9	10.3
Social security contributions	4.7	9.7	5.9	5.2
Customs duties	—	0.5	0.7	—
Other	—	0.2	1.0	0.9

Sources: IMF staff estimates; and data from national authorities.
[1]Includes profit remittances and taxes on production.
[2]Including amortization transfers to the budget.

The tax system was reviewed and revised at the end of each five-year plan, as part of the general revision of the regulatory system that included prices and exchange rates. The effect of the decline in the administratively set prices in the last 20 years was to reduce the tax base, particularly with respect to enterprise profits, because of the more pronounced decline in wholesale prices compared with retail prices. This explains the increased weight of turnover taxes, and the reduced weight of enterprise taxes over time.

As in other CPEs[31] most of the tax revenue in Albania comes from taxes on enterprises: transfer of profits and amortization funds, and turnover taxes. However, a cross-country comparison (Table 17) also reveals some special characteristics of the Albanian tax system. First, Albania has relied more extensively than other CPEs on the turnover tax, probably because of the adverse impact of administrative price declines on enterprise profitability. Second, Albania was the only country in which the share of amortization transfers (grouped together with profit transfers in Table 17) was still important. Third, although in most CPEs the income redistribution role of tax policy was limited, it did not exist at all in Albania. Finally, there were no customs duties in Albania until very recently.

---

[31]The analysis here focuses on comparing economies at the same stage of economic reforms, that is, those that started reforms recently. For this reason, reforming CPEs such as Hungary, Poland, or Yugoslavia are excluded from the comparison.

Expenditures[32]

The share of expenditure in GDP, averaging about 54 percent, does not fully reflect the extent of state intervention.[33] Its structure illustrates the highly centralized nature of the economy, with investment accounting for roughly half of total expenditure (Tables A13 and A14).[34] Subsidies to enterprises were also relatively high throughout the 1980s, averaging 7 percent of GDP in 1982–90, and reaching over 14 percent in 1990. The government wage bill during the 1980s, at about 6–7 percent of GDP, was comparable to countries at a similar stage of development. The level of other current expenditures was relatively low, reflecting very low interest payments on foreign debt and low outlays on operation and maintenance. (A part of gross investment may also be associated with operation and maintenance expenditures.) Finally, the share of social security payments in total expenditure increased steadily through the 1980s, reaching almost 14 percent in 1990.

Public investment (41 percent of total expenditure in 1990) accounted for most of the investment in the economy. It averaged around 28 percent of

---

[32]Refers to total expenditure in the consolidated budget.
[33]Although difficult to quantify, state intervention has been pervasive through discretionary regulatory policies as well as through exclusive state ownership of enterprises and land. Excluding the agricultural sector, both the expenditure and the tax to GDP ratio (excluding agriculture) would be much higher, the latter close to 60 percent.
[34]Gross investment, as it appears in the budget.

GDP in 1982–85, and declined slightly to below 27 percent of GDP in 1986–90 (Tables A13 and A14). During the 1980s, investment for the material sphere accounted for about 75–80 percent of the total, of which half was directed to heavy industry (energy and mining), a fourth to agriculture, and a tenth to housing and local services. Investment in light industry was small, accounting for only 4–5 percent of overall investment in the material sphere. Investment in the nonmaterial sphere was dominated by outlays for defense, representing 80–85 percent of total nonmaterial investment. Investment for health, education, and culture was about 1 percent of GDP.

Subsidies were another important expenditure item during the 1980s, with their share in total expenditures averaging about 14 percent during 1982–89 before jumping to 25 percent in 1990. This category includes consumer (or price) subsidies, transfers to the State Agricultural Bank, and enterprise subsidies. Consumer subsidies were relatively stable over the 1980s, ranging between 1.3 percent and 2.2 percent of GDP, reflecting fixed prices and unchanged private consumption of subsidized goods. These subsidies are provided mainly for cereals, meat—which together account for about two thirds of all price subsidies—and fertilizers (Table A15). Transfers to the State Agricultural Bank were to cover losses related to long-term credit to agricultural cooperatives. Enterprise subsidies (Table A16) were of different types and reached more than 14 percent of GDP in 1990. The most important were those to cover losses, which accounted for 40 percent of total enterprise subsidies in 1982–89; their share jumped to 75 percent in 1990. Subsidies for increases in working capital accounted for a share of about 18 percent, while foreign trade and price subsidies in agriculture each account for a share of 14 percent.

The share of *wages and salaries* in total outlays were relatively stable at 12–13 percent in the 1980s (Table A13). Between 1982 and 1990, the wage bill rose by a cumulative 22 percent, reflecting increases in general government employment, as the average wage in the sector increased only by a cumulative 3.5 percent.

In the 1980s, expenditure on *interest payments* was limited, reflecting the virtual lack of foreign debt following Albania's unilateral cancellation of most of its debt in 1978 and the interest-free nature of domestic debt.

Social security expenditures almost doubled over the 1980s, reaching a level of 8.8 percent of GDP in 1990, and a share of 14 percent of total expenditure in the same year. Pensions were the single most important reason, accounting for about 80 percent of the total. There are three pension categories: regular retirement pensions, family pensions for families without an adult wage earner, and disability pensions. In addition, maternity allowance and sick pay are provided. Virtually all social benefits are wage related; some are subject to minimum and maximum limits. After modest surpluses in the 1960s and 1970s, the social security system started to incur deficits in the early 1980s. The deficit rose from 1 percent of GDP in 1982 to more than 2 percent by 1985. It was kept below 2 percent of GDP in 1986–87 following an increase in the contribution rates, and rose again after 1987 in the wake of sizable increases in expenditures.

Comparison with other prereform CPEs reveals a similar level but a somewhat different structure of expenditure. As Table 18 indicates, with the exception of Romania, the levels of expenditure were similar in all CPEs. The lower expenditures in Romania could be explained by the partial inclusion of the social security system in the budget. Gross capital outlays[35] were markedly higher in Albania than in the other CPEs, reflecting relatively greater centralization in its industrialization effort. Enterprise subsidies, generally high in all four countries, were lowest in Albania, since the primary instruments for determining enterprise income were pricing and taxation policy rather than subsidization. The lower social security outlays in Albania may have reflected the country's lower level of economic development.

Deficit Financing

As explained earlier, fiscal deficits were financed mainly by drawdowns of government deposits with the central bank. The deposits in the Reserve Fund, after peaking at leks 3.3 billion (21 percent of GDP) in 1980, fell to leks 827 million (5 percent of GDP) by the end of 1990. In addition, other accounts such as those of the branch ministries and the Reserve Fund of the Council of Ministers (denominated in foreign exchange) with the central bank, as well as the proceeds from the sale of the strategic commodity reserves, occasionally financed the deficit. The Government also used short-term credit through an overdraft facility on its transaction accounts with the central bank, and advances, mainly to cover foreign trade

---

[35]The comparison of the structure of expenditure may be biased by including outlays for operation and maintenance in Albania, while some capital outlays in Czechoslovakia and Bulgaria are included in the operation and maintenance category. To account for these classification differences, expenditure on capital and operation and maintenance is combined in Table 18 and shown as a memorandum item.

Table 18. Structure of Government Expenditure, 1985
(In percent of GDP)

	Albania	Bulgaria	Czechoslovakia	Romania
Total expenditure	52.7	55.2	57.3	43.4[1]
Current expenditure	26.2	47.4	46.3	26.8
Wage bill	6.7	4.6	6.8	4.3
Interest payments	0.2	0.8	—	1.3
Operation and maintenance	4.7	14.5	12.8	5.0
Price subsidies	1.9	1.5	3.9	0.1
Enterprise subsidies[2]	5.4	11.3	7.9	9.4[3]
Social security outlays	6.1	10.1	12.5	6.7[1]
Other	—	4.7	2.1	—
Capital expenditure and net lending	26.5[4]	7.8	11.3	16.6
Memorandum item:				
Capital outlay, operation and maintenance	31.2	26.3	25.1	21.6

Sources: IMF staff estimates; and data from national authorities.
[1]Social security in the budget contains only pensions and allocations for children; other social insurance is outside the budget.
[2]Including foreign trade subsidies.
[3]Including losses associated with agricultural debt reductions.
[4]Gross investment, including use of funds of branch ministries and the Council of Ministers.

losses. In recent times, the Government also incurred significant arrears to the enterprise sector.

Interaction of Ministry of Finance with State Enterprises

In Albania, as in other CPEs, the revenue and expenditure sides of the budget are dominated by transactions with enterprises. However, the distinction between government accounts and those of enterprises can be blurred. For example, the Government had the authority to confiscate enterprise deposits without notice, or to freeze the account of an enterprise that had failed to pay its taxes.

Although the basic nature of the links between the Government and the enterprise sector did not change until the introduction of the "new economic mechanism" in 1990, their financial relationship underwent a distinct change during the 1980s (Table A17). In particular, transfers from the enterprise sector in the form of profit and amortization transfers and confiscation of enterprise deposits increased from 18.9 percent of GDP in 1982 to over 21 percent of GDP in 1984–85. However, these transfers dropped sharply to 17.2 percent of GDP in 1986, and 16.4 percent in 1989, reaching 13.1 percent of GDP in 1990. On the other hand, subsidies to the enterprise sector were relatively stable at around 5 percent of GDP

until 1988, when they rose to 6.8 percent, and peaked at 14.3 percent of GDP in 1990.

These trends translated into a relatively stable net contribution to the budget by the enterprise sector between 1982 and 1985, averaging around 15 percent of GDP per annum. However, the net contribution fell in 1986 to 13 percent of GDP, and gradually declined to 9.7 percent of GDP by 1989. In 1990, the jump in enterprise subsidies, together with a further drop in enterprise transfers to the budget, led to a net flow of resources from the budget to the enterprises, at least on a commitment basis. The trend of declining net contributions by enterprises reflected a pronounced worsening in the profitability of the enterprise sector, owing to their low efficiency.

Money and Credit

The Financial System

The *banking system* in Albania is composed of the State Bank of Albania, the State Agricultural Bank, the Albanian Commercial Bank (formerly Albanian State Bank for Foreign Relations), and a network of savings bank branches.

The State Bank of Albania (SBA) performs both central banking and commercial banking functions (Table A18). In its central banking capacity, it issues currency, acts as banker to the Government, contributes to the formulation and implementation of monetary policy, provides funds to the State Agricultural Bank, and, until the creation of the Albanian State Bank for Foreign Relations in December 1990, held all of the country's foreign exchange assets and liabilities, including gold held on behalf of the Government. The SBA transfers most of its profits to the state budget and, as the fiscal agent for the Government, makes payments to individuals and nonagricultural state enterprises, and collects all government revenues. The SBA's commercial banking activities mainly involve acceptance of deposits from, and provision of credits to, nonagricultural state enterprises to finance their operating expenses.[36] The SBA also provides a small amount of housing credit to individuals and, since January 1991, has granted credit for the establishment of private sector businesses in the small-scale handicraft and services sectors.

The State Agricultural Bank (SAB) was created in 1970 from a department of the SBA specializing in agricultural financial operations. The SAB is the sole lender to state farms and cooperatives[37] and holds their deposits (Table A19). It is also funded by transfers from the SBA and the government budget.[38] The SAB provides loans to individuals for housing in rural areas and, since January 1991, credits to individuals to establish small rural businesses. It also acts as fiscal agent of the Government in making payments to state farms and cooperatives.

Throughout the country, there is a network of nearly 40,000 savings bank local representatives, which collect deposits (not insured) and insurance premiums from individuals, and redeposit all of these funds with the SBA (Table A20). The savings banks were authorized to make loans only in late 1991.

The Albanian Commercial Bank (ACB) began operating as a separate bank on January 1, 1991 under the name Albanian State Bank for Foreign

Relations. The new bank was created from the Foreign Relations Department of the SBA with the objective of taking over the commercial foreign exchange transactions with state enterprises and individuals previously conducted by the SBA. The ACB holds the bilateral balances of the countries of the former CMEA, which were previously in the balance sheet of the SBA, and a small portion of the country's foreign exchange reserves. It is authorized to borrow abroad in its own name. The SBA is responsible for providing ACB's capital and reserves, but the transfer of these funds had not taken place as of end-1991.

There are no other financial institutions, money or bond markets, or stock exchange in Albania. Interbank transactions are limited to the routine redepositing of funds by the savings banks at the SBA, and the transfer of funds from the SBA to the SAB. Interenterprise credit is not permitted and there is no evidence that it has taken place.

The *payments system* in Albania has involved only transactions in cash and clearing of invoices presented to banks. There are no checks or checking accounts for transactions in leks, though checks are used by individuals for some foreign exchange transactions. Most cash transactions are carried out by the household sector, as wage and personal consumption payments occur in this form. Clearing of invoices is used in transactions among public enterprises and between these enterprises and the Government. Invoices presented for payment by state enterprises lacking adequate funds are cleared by the SBA, usually with attendant debiting of accounts in the form of credit arrears.[39]

Monetary and Credit Policies

Although monetary and credit policies played a passive macroeconomic role, they were an integral part of Albania's state planning process. Decisions on the quantity and allocation of credit needed to implement the state plan were made at the beginning of each year by the Council of Ministers, based on joint recommendations made by the Ministry of Finance, the State Planning Commission, and the SBA. The annual credit programs included

---

[36]Until 1990, virtually all deposits at the SBA were denominated in domestic currency. Since 1988, the SBA has held a limited amount of household deposits denominated in foreign currency (equal to 0.3 percent of the stock of domestic currency deposits at end-1990), which resulted from transfers from abroad.

Since 1987, the SBA has also provided a limited amount of investment credits to state enterprises.

[37]The SAB's stock of outstanding credits at end-1990 was distributed between working capital credit to both state farms and cooperatives (75 percent) and investment credits to the cooperatives (25 percent).

[38]Most of its liabilities to the Government were written off in March 1991 to allow the SAB in turn to write off almost one third of its outstanding loans to cooperatives.

---

[39]Arrears, most of which result from delays in settlements by the Government, have been a normal part of the financial arrangements between the state enterprises and the SBA, but became particularly prominent in 1990 when the stock of unpaid SBA credit to state enterprises was equivalent to over 9 percent of total credit extended to them. State enterprises' arrears to the SBA are usually settled when budgetary funds become available prior to the closure of the budget accounts. Similar arrangements apply to arrears incurred by the state farms and the cooperatives to the SAB.

details of the projected financing requirements of the state budget, and the bank credit needed to meet the financing requirements of the state enterprises, the state farms, and the cooperatives. There was only limited allowance for credit to households, mainly for small mortgage loans. Credit policy has been implemented by the SBA and the specialized banks. During the year, the SBA was authorized to make appropriate adjustments to approved credit policies in response to deviations from plan targets, and at times the SBA used its authority in this area to support economic activity.[40] The SBA also reviews the level and structure of interest rates on deposits and loans and proposes changes to the Council of Ministers. However, the rare changes in interest rates are indicative of their minor role as an instrument of monetary policy. Except for interest rates on foreign currency deposits, all interest rates were kept constant throughout 1980–90, reflecting their limited allocative role in the context of the central plan (Tables A21 and A22). All interest rates were positive in real terms when evaluated in terms of changes in official retail prices. With the emphasis placed on direct control of credit and the requirement that the savings banks place surplus funds at the SBA, the authorities have seen no need to introduce reserve requirements.

Ceilings on the maximum amount of currency issued are established from time to time by the Council of Ministers, based on proposals by the SBA. Within the established ceilings, the SBA issues currency, as needed, to allow the Government and the public enterprises to make cash payments (mainly for wages) and to satisfy the household sector's demands for cash balances. Like government departments, enterprises and banks are required to place all surplus funds at the SBA, and virtually all currency in circulation in Albania is held by households.

Monetary Developments[41]

In 1980–88, broad money increased by an average of 5 percent a year, compared with an average annual growth of nominal GDP of 1.1 percent

(Table 19). Year-to-year fluctuations in the rate of broad money expansion were generally moderate, and largely the result of SBA financing of the Central Government, mainly by drawing down government deposits in the Reserve Fund account. Short-term fluctuations in credit to the rest of the economy also had some effect on broad money, but the longer-term growth of such credit was low, averaging 1.3 percent a year. With an average annual increase in net foreign assets of 0.7 percent, movements in the foreign balance had only a minor effect on Albania's monetary developments until 1987. In that year, the growth of broad money was due to a combination of higher budget deficit financing and rising credit to public enterprises to finance, inter alia, their increased holdings of raw material stocks, partly acquired from the government strategic commodity reserves.[42] In 1988, working capital credits to state enterprises decreased, and there was a drain of liquidity caused by a substantial decline in net foreign assets (Table 19).

In 1989, a year in which output recovered strongly, the expansion of broad money (14.8 percent) reflected an acceleration of domestic credit (to a rate of 21.5 percent, from a contraction of 0.7 percent in 1988), only partially offset by the loss of liquidity through the balance of payments. The growth of domestic credit resulted from an increase in bank credit to the Government (leks 910 million, equivalent to 23.1 percent of the stock of broad money at the beginning of the year)[43] and a 5.4 percent increase in credit to the economy, mostly to state enterprises and to state farms to finance their increased holdings of stocks of raw materials. The enlarged balance of payments deficit that accompanied the economic recovery resulted in a deterioration (leks 920 million) in the net foreign asset position. Gross foreign assets rose by leks 2.1

---

[40]This was particularly apparent in 1990, when the state enterprises' liquidity was severely tightened by the emergence of large arrears in government payments.

[41]In interpreting the banking system's financial accounts, several characteristics of the official data should be noted. First, the position of the Government at the SBA covers the principal operating account of the state budget (the Reserve Fund account), other government accounts that fall within the scope of the Central Government's budgetary operations, and gold and precious metals held by the SBA on behalf of the Government. Second, insufficient information is available to

distinguish clearly between time and savings deposits held by public enterprises as well as households, and between those deposits that are freely usable by depositors and those whose use is restricted by government regulation and approval procedures. These problems ruled out the accurate compilation of conventionally defined aggregates for narrow money and quasi-money.

[42]In 1987 and 1988, there were net sales of raw materials and consumer goods from the strategic commodity reserves, which were stocks administered by some state enterprises, directly controlled by the Prime Minister. These emergency reserve stocks were sold to ease poor supply conditions. The proceeds from these transactions (leks 650 million in 1987 and leks 120 million in 1988), at first to be used to replenish the stocks, were subsequently transferred to the budget where they appear as nontax revenues. Owing to their specific nature, the corresponding amounts were treated in the monetary accounts as restricted deposits.

[43]Excluding revaluations, the flow of credit to the Government was leks 1,029 million.

Table 19. Monetary Survey, 1980–90
(In millions of leks; end of period)

	1980	1981	1982	1983	1984	1985	1986	1987	1988	1989	1990
ASSETS											
Net foreign assets	473.5	448.9	498.1	434.4	405.2	451.2	487.5	497.7	150.2	−769.7	−2,723.6
Foreign assets	630.5	708.1	666.9	546.0	513.5	529.5	630.8	720.6	1,540.2	3,645.2	1,961.1
Foreign liabilities[1]	157.0	259.2	168.8	111.6	108.3	78.3	143.3	222.8	1,390.0	4,414.9	4,684.8
Total domestic credit	3,836.1	4,341.2	4,551.4	5,130.3	5,139.7	5,505.2	5,696.5	6,428.4	6,381.4	7,754.0	9,452.9
To government (net)	−3,951.4	−3,895.0	−4,014.3	−3,345.9	−2,968.0	−2,559.7	−2,523.1	−2,274.8	−2,246.4	−1,336.3	−651.2
To the economy	7,787.5	8,236.3	8,565.6	8,476.3	8,107.7	8,064.9	8,219.5	8,703.3	8,627.8	9,090.3	10,104.1
State enterprises	5,865.0	6,168.0	6,438.9	6,377.2	5,901.4	5,873.1	5,626.1	5,926.4	5,711.2	6,000.0	6,671.2
State farms	689.0	677.0	710.0	712.0	765.0	800.0	993.0	1,085.0	1,175.0	1,317.0	1,538.0
Cooperatives	1,127.0	1,284.0	1,306.0	1,271.0	1,318.0	1,260.0	1,458.0	1,536.0	1,573.0	1,590.0	1,700.0
Households	106.5	107.3	110.8	116.1	123.2	131.8	142.5	155.9	168.6	183.4	194.9
LIABILITIES											
Broad money	2,670.2	2,703.6	2,688.2	2,980.0	3,045.0	3,173.0	3,403.4	3,646.9	3,931.3	4,514.4	5,464.2
Currency in circulation	703.3	757.3	800.2	911.2	944.5	967.1	1,035.2	1,162.4	1,233.9	1,241.7	1,694.9
Deposits[2]	1,966.9	1,946.3	1,888.0	2,068.8	2,100.5	2,205.9	2,368.2	2,484.5	2,697.4	3,272.7	3,769.4
Domestic currency deposits	1,966.9	1,946.3	1,888.0	2,068.8	2,100.5	2,205.9	2,368.2	2,484.5	2,696.7	3,270.5	3,758.9
State enterprises	1,000.9	894.3	752.0	817.8	785.5	704.9	834.2	777.5	879.7	1,278.5	1,588.9
State farms	62.0	69.0	73.0	96.0	75.0	69.0	65.0	78.0	83.0	76.0	104.0
Cooperatives	204.0	248.0	275.0	264.0	255.0	361.0	286.0	300.0	256.0	349.0	359.0
Households' demand deposits	405.0	415.0	445.0	507.0	558.0	606.0	670.0	755.0	832.0	864.0	917.0
Households' time deposits	295.0	320.0	343.0	384.0	427.0	465.0	513.0	574.0	646.0	703.0	790.0
Foreign currency deposits	—	—	—	—	—	—	—	—	0.7	2.2	10.5
Other items (net)	1,639.4	2,086.6	2,361.3	2,584.7	2,499.9	2,783.4	2,780.6	3,279.3	2,600.3	2,469.9	1,265.0
Capital and reserves	1,250.0	1,250.0	1,250.0	1,250.0	1,250.0	1,250.0	1,250.0	1,250.0	1,250.0	1,250.0	1,250.0
Other identified items	906.1	1,212.8	1,270.2	1,182.8	936.1	1,014.3	1,043.9	1,614.9	1,001.9	1,440.2	−496.5
Unidentified items	−516.7	−376.2	−158.9	152.0	313.9	519.0	486.7	414.4	348.4	−220.3	511.5
Vertical check	—	—	—	—	—	—	—	—	—	—	—
Memorandum items:											
Narrow money[3]	1,108.3	1,172.3	1,245.2	1,418.2	1,502.5	1,573.1	1,705.2	1,917.4	2,065.9	2,105.7	2,611.9
Domestic credit to government (net), excluding revaluations	−3,951.4	−3,895.0	−4,014.3	−3,345.9	−2,968.0	−2,447.0	−2,410.3	−2,162.1	−2,133.6	−1,104.6	−331.2

Sources: State Bank of Albania; and IMF staff calculations.

[1]Including arrears.

[2]Time and demand deposits of state enterprises, state farms, and cooperatives cannot be separated on the basis of the information available. Their liquidity is de facto constrained and not comparable to international standards.

[3]Sum of currency in circulation and households' demand deposits. Since the liquidity of households' demand deposits is de facto limited, the definition of narrow money adopted here is not comparable to international standards.

billion, owing entirely to the redepositing abroad of convertible currency deposits by foreign commercial banks at the SBA.

Despite the strong decline in output and the increasing scarcity of consumer goods, a further acceleration of liquidity growth took place in 1990. The balance of payments continued to deteriorate, but broad money increased by 21 percent and narrow money (currency plus households' demand deposits), virtually unchanged in 1989, rose by 24 percent, largely on account of the strong increase in currency in circulation (Table 19). Bank financing of the 1990 budget deficit and credit to the public enterprises (ostensibly to ease the liquidity squeeze caused by budgetary arrears) were the principal factors behind a 22 percent increase in domestic credit. Bank credit to the Government amounted to leks 0.7 billion (15.2 percent of the stock of broad money at the beginning of the year).[44] Credit to the economy rose by 11.2 percent, reflecting bank lending to support the implementation of the plan as a result of delays in the transfer of funds from the Government.[45] By end-1990, the Government's domestic arrears related to its 1990 budget operations amounted to approximately leks 1.9 billion.

Albania's net foreign assets declined by leks 2.0 billion during 1990. The deterioration in the net foreign asset position during 1990 was due to a large reduction in gross foreign assets that reflected both financing of the enlarged balance of payments deficit and losses arising from the SBA's trading transactions in European gold and foreign exchange markets. Moreover, about half of the SBA's gross foreign asset holdings represented deposits held by correspondent banks against Albania's future obligations. With the continued decline in gross foreign assets in the first quarter of 1991, virtually all of Albania's foreign assets were not usable. In 1990, foreign liabilities of the banking system rose owing to the accumulation of arrears in payments to foreign commercial banks.

Household Financial Assets and Liabilities

During the 1980s, bank claims on households rose moderately, from 0.7 percent of GDP in 1980 to 1.2 percent in 1990 (Chart 10). In contrast, holdings of currency and bank deposits by households rose from 9 percent of GDP in 1980 to 21 percent in 1990. The accumulation of liquid assets

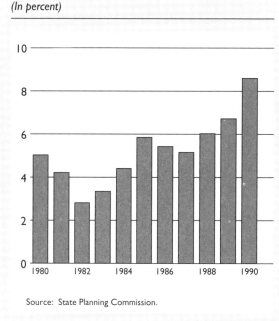

Chart 7. Unemployment Rate, 1980–90
(In percent)

Source: State Planning Commission.

continuously increased from 1980 to 1988, recording a slowdown in 1989 (a year of solid economic growth, particularly in the agricultural sector), and then strongly accelerated during 1990.

The accumulation of household liquid assets in 1980–90 appears to have been closely related to the persistent rationing and the increasingly severe constraints on the availability of consumer goods in the official markets, as well as to the limited development of parallel goods markets. In addition, households had a very limited range of investment opportunities, as purchases of real assets were banned (with minor exceptions for rural housing), and no other financial assets were available.

The accumulation of household liquid assets in 1980–88 was closely correlated to the indicator of excess demand registered at the retail stores.[46] In 1989, a strong recovery in agricultural and industrial production led to a sharp increase in the supply of consumer goods, the growth of expenditure at retail stores matched the rise in total incomes, and there was little change in household financial savings. In 1990, when a sharp decline in production caused renewed and severe shortages of consumer goods, household financial savings rose by over 21 percent. They accelerated further in the

---

[44]Excluding revaluations, the flow of credit to the Government was about leks 773 million.

[45]Credit to state enterprises included some leks 400 million in the form of overdrafts to enterprises that had insufficient funds to settle payments obligations.

[46]The coefficient of linear correlation between this indicator and household liquid assets equaled 0.92 for the period.

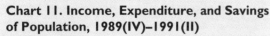

Chart 11. Income, Expenditure, and Savings of Population, 1989(IV)–1991(II)
(In millions of leks)

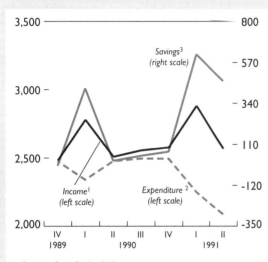

Source: State Bank of Albania.
[1]Sum of wages, social security payments, and other incomes.
[2]Sum of expenditure on goods, services, and other items.
[3]Computed as the difference of income and expenditure in each quarter. When cumulated over the sample period, savings match the sum of the changes in the stock of currency in circulation and household deposits.

Chart 12. Distribution of Household Bank Deposits, 1985 and 1990
(Shares in percent)

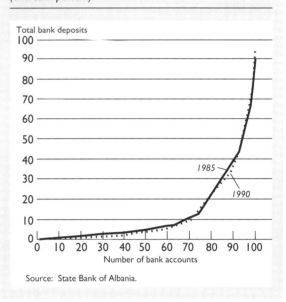

Source: State Bank of Albania.

first half of 1991, as the rise in nominal incomes following an upward adjustment of wages was accompanied by a marked decline in expenditure (Chart 11) owing to an increasing scarcity of commodities.

Available data indicate that household bank deposits were highly concentrated (Chart 12). At end-1990, almost 12 percent of the total stock of deposits was accounted for by only 0.4 percent of bank accounts holding over leks 30,000 (about six times the 1990 level of per capita income), and 65 percent of total deposits by less than 11 percent of bank accounts holding over leks 5,000 (approximately the 1990 level of per capita income).

Balance of Payments and External Issues

Albania can be characterized as a relatively closed economy and as an exporter of primary commodities. The ratio of the average of exports and imports to GDP during the 1980s was in the range of 15–20 percent, which was similar to the range in Poland and Romania, but considerably smaller than that in Bulgaria, Czechoslovakia, Hungary, and Yugoslavia (a range of 35–40 percent).

Overview of External Developments

From the Second World War to the late 1970s, Albania's trading partners were predominantly other socialist countries. After 1961, when Albania interrupted financial relations with the U.S.S.R. and left the CMEA, China became its major trading partner, and provided most of the substantial foreign credits that during the 1960s and 1970s financed large balance of payments deficits in nonconvertible currencies (Chart 13). In 1978, Albania's external relations were altered substantially when a policy of "autarky" and "self-sufficiency" was implemented. Over most of the following decade, trade was increasingly oriented toward the convertible currency area (Chart 14), the current account in convertible currencies (Table 20) registered small deficits financed by a rundown in foreign exchange reserves accumulated over the 1970s, and that in nonconvertible currencies was broadly balanced (Tables A23 and A24). During this period, Albania benefited from improving terms of trade and incurred practically no foreign debt.

In recent years, Albania's external position deteriorated markedly, as its terms of trade weakened sharply in 1990, drought and production-related problems in domestic supply reduced exports and increased imports, and access to export markets in Eastern Europe was disrupted. There was also pressure for increased imports of consumer goods as the economic and political reforms were instituted in 1990 and 1991. The current account defi-

Chart 13. Current Account Balance, 1968–90
(In millions of U.S. dollars)

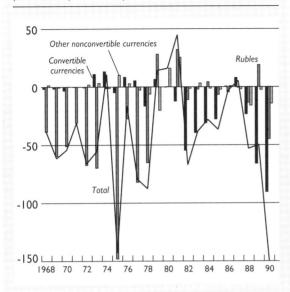

Chart 14. Exports and Imports, 1968–90
(In millions of U.S. dollars)

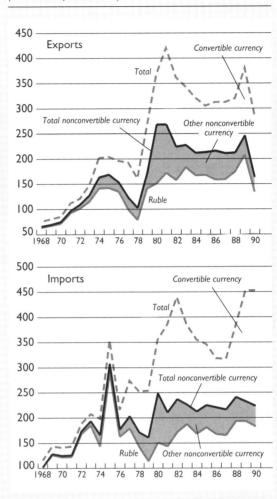

cit in convertible currencies widened substantially, as did that in nonconvertible currencies in 1990, reflecting a deterioration in terms of trade in convertible currencies and a sharp increase in the volume of convertible currency imports. The large trade deficit in nonconvertible currencies in 1990 reflected both structural changes in export markets in Eastern Europe and a shift of exports from the nonconvertible to the convertible currency area because of the need to earn convertible currencies. Moreover, during 1988–90 lack of control over the management of external reserves resulted in losses from foreign exchange speculation amounting to 10 percent of GDP. The overall balance of payments deficits were financed by the near exhaustion of foreign reserves (including the sale of gold reserves), external borrowing, arrears on external trade payments and interbank borrowing, and defaults on foreign exchange transactions. Although Albania had practically no international debt, in a few years it managed to build up a significant and difficult external debt problem. Total external debt, including debt associated with the financing of the current account deficit in nonconvertible currencies, had increased to about $500 million (30 percent of GDP) by June 1991, two thirds of which was accounted for by payments arrears.

Foreign Trade

The volume, composition, and direction of Albania's trade changed considerably during the

1970s and 1980s. The volume of exports (Table A25) increased substantially in the 1970s with increases in the production and export of petroleum products, chrome ore, and electrical energy. In the 1980s production and export of petroleum fell sharply and there were larger exports of chrome and tobacco. Total trade has remained a fairly small percentage of GDP, with exports and imports equivalent to 14 percent and 22 percent of GDP, respectively, in 1990.

Foreign trade was characterized by a relatively large share of manufactured goods and machinery and, more recently, imports of food and live animals, and a high proportion of raw material exports (Tables A26 and A27). Exports of food, beverages and tobacco, crude materials, and mineral fuels and related products (Standard International Trade Classification—SITC 0–3) accounted for the major part of exports in nonconvertible

Table 20. Balance of Payments in Convertible Currencies, 1968–91
(In millions of U.S. dollars)

	1968	1969	1970	1971	1972	1973	1974	1975	1976	1977	1978	1979	1980	1981	1982	1983	1984	1985	1986	1987	1988	1989	1990	1991 Jan.–June Estimate
Current account	−1.6	−1.4	−3.2	−0.2	−0.6	10.9	13.2	−4.8	8.4	5.3	−16.4	6.5	0.2	−12.3	−54.6	−39.4	−31.1	−27.8	0.5	7.8	−23.5	−70.4	−95.1	−93.2
Trade balance	−3.6	−3.6	−5.3	−2.1	−3.1	6.4	6.7	−11.0	4.3	0.1	−22.0	1.2	−6.0	−22.7	−65.2	−43.0	−33.6	−28.7	−0.6	1.0	−34.8	−90.9	−109.6	−78.7
Exports, f.o.b.	9.1	10.2	9.3	14.2	10.7	18.7	37.5	33.9	41.8	68.9	57.5	92.4	99.1	150.5	136.3	114.3	107.9	91.2	95.5	100.3	106.6	132.7	123.0	41.3
Imports, f.o.b.	12.7	13.8	14.6	16.3	13.8	12.3	30.8	44.9	37.5	68.8	79.5	91.3	105.1	173.2	201.5	157.3	141.5	119.9	96.1	99.3	141.4	223.6	232.6	120.0
Services balance	−0.3	−0.4	−0.3	−0.5	−0.6	0.5	0.5	−0.1	0.5	2.2	2.1	1.3	3.3	3.3	4.1	−2.4	−3.9	−4.9	−4.7	−0.1	4.3	9.9	−0.4	−14.5
Receipts	0.9	1.0	1.2	1.3	1.4	2.3	2.4	1.9	4.6	5.8	6.7	8.8	10.5	15.5	18.6	11.4	8.4	5.5	6.6	12.48	19.1	28.4	21.2	5.3
Shipment and other transportation	0.3	0.3	0.2	0.3	0.2	0.6	0.3	0.1	0.2	0.6	0.1	0.3	—	1.0	0.3	0.3	0.1	0.1	0.6	0.8	0.9	1.0	1.1	—
Travel	0.1	0.1	0.2	0.2	0.3	0.4	0.4	0.5	0.5	0.4	0.4	0.5	0.7	1.0	0.5	0.5	0.6	0.6	1.1	2.0	3.0	3.3	3.5	—
Interest	0.6	0.6	0.8	0.8	1.0	1.4	1.7	1.3	2.8	3.2	4.4	5.4	7.4	12.0	14.7	7.7	4.3	2.3	0.8	1.1	0.9	0.4	…	…
Other	1.2	1.4	1.5	1.9	2.1	1.8	2.0	2.0	3.0	3.6	4.6	7.5	10.4	12.2	14.5	13.8	12.3	10.4	11.3	12.5	14.8	23.7	16.6	16.8
Expenditures	1.2	1.4	1.5	1.9	2.1	1.8	2.0	2.0	3.0	3.6	4.6	7.5	10.4	12.2	14.5	13.8	12.3	10.4	11.3	12.5	14.8	18.5	21.6	16.8
Shipment and other transportation	0.3	0.3	0.3	0.5	0.1	0.3	0.3	0.3	0.5	1.5	1.7	3.3	5.4	5.5	7.3	6.7	4.8	2.7	3.8	3.6	4.9	7.0	6.1	1.8
Insurance	0.1	0.1	0.1	0.1	0.1	0.1	0.2	0.2	0.2	0.3	0.4	0.5	0.5	0.9	1.0	0.8	0.7	0.6	0.5	0.5	0.7	1.1	1.1	—
Interest	—	—	—	—	—	—	—	—	—	1.8	2.5	3.8	4.5	5.8	6.2	6.3	6.8	7.1	7.0	8.4	9.2	10.4	12.7	—
Other	0.8	1.0	1.1	1.3	1.9	1.5	1.5	1.5	1.8	3.1	3.6	4.1	5.8	7.1	6.5	6.0	6.5	5.7	5.7	6.9	7.0	9.1	15.0	7.0
Unrequited transfers, net	2.3	2.6	2.4	2.5	3.1	4.0	6.0	6.3	3.1	3.1	3.6	4.0	5.8	7.1	6.5	6.0	6.5	5.7	5.7	6.9	7.0	9.1	15.0	15.0
Private	2.3	2.6	2.4	2.5	3.1	4.0	6.0	6.3	3.1	3.1	3.6	4.1	5.8	7.1	6.5	6.0	6.5	5.7	5.7	6.9	7.0	9.1	15.0	15.0
Receipts	2.3	2.6	2.4	2.5	3.1	4.0	6.0	6.3	3.1	3.1	3.6	4.1	5.8	7.1	6.5	6.0	6.5	5.7	5.7	6.9	7.0	9.1	15.0	15.0
Payments	—	—	—	—	—	—	—	—	—	—	—	—	—	—	—	—	—	—	—	—	—	—	—	—
Official	—	—	—	—	—	—	—	—	—	—	—	—	—	—	—	—	—	—	—	—	—	1.5	—	—
Capital account	—	10.0	8.6	11.4	10.4	8.4	3.9	12.7	−2.7	1.2	−0.2	−2.5	1.7	5.7	7.7	−7.4	3.5	2.2	−5.6	−3.6	9.8	14.8	56.6	15.0
Medium- and long-term, net	—	10.0	8.6	9.3	6.8	13.4	7.1	7.4	—	—	—	—	—	—	—	—	—	—	—	—	—	—	29.1	—
Credits received	—	10.0	8.6	9.3	6.8	13.4	7.1	7.4	—	—	—	—	—	—	—	—	—	—	—	—	—	—	29.1	—
Disbursements	—	10.0	8.6	9.3	6.8	13.4	7.1	7.4	—	—	—	—	—	—	—	—	—	—	—	—	—	—	29.1	—
Repayments	—	—	—	—	—	—	—	—	—	—	—	—	—	—	—	—	—	—	—	—	—	—	—	—
Credits extended	—	—	—	—	—	—	—	—	—	—	—	—	—	—	—	—	—	—	—	—	—	—	—	—
Short-term capital, net	1.3	—	—	2.1	3.6	−5.0	−3.2	5.3	−2.7	1.2	−0.2	−2.5	1.7	5.7	7.7	−7.4	3.5	2.2	−5.6	−3.6	9.8	14.8	27.5	15.0
Errors and omissions	1.3	−2.4	−3.8	−11.3	−6.4	−7.6	−2.9	−0.9	0.9	13.0	−8.6	7.9	−14.1	14.7	14.1	5.9	15.4	7.8	5.1	9.8	22.8	−4.0	10.1	−1.3
Overall balance	−0.2	6.2	1.6	−0.1	3.3	11.8	14.1	7.0	6.5	19.6	−25.2	11.9	−12.6	8.1	−32.8	−40.9	−12.2	−17.8	−0.1	14.0	9.1	−59.6	−28.4	−79.5
Financing of overall balance	0.2	−6.2	−1.6	0.1	−3.3	−11.8	−14.1	−7.0	−6.5	−19.6	25.2	−11.9	12.6	−8.1	32.8	40.9	12.2	17.8	0.1	−14.0	−9.1	59.6	28.4	79.5
Change in reserves —, increase	0.2	−6.2	−1.6	0.1	−3.3	−11.8	−14.1	−7.0	−6.5	−15.3	11.9	−9.6	−3.4	−26.1	13.4	41.3	12.0	17.6	1.4	−11.7	−130.6	−264.1	206.3	206.6
Settlement of clearing account balances	—	—	—	—	—	—	—	—	—	−4.3	13.3	−2.3	13.9	16.3	21.2	−0.8	—	−0.4	—	−3.1	−6.9	−16.8	−10.4	—
Profit from gold sales	—	—	—	—	—	—	—	—	—	—	—	—	—	—	—	—	—	—	—	—	23.6	13.7	31.4	—
Increase in arrears	—	—	—	—	—	—	—	—	—	—	—	—	—	—	—	—	—	—	—	—	—	—	—	—
Increase in foreign deposits	—	—	—	—	—	—	—	—	—	—	—	—	2.0	1.7	−1.7	0.4	0.2	0.6	−1.3	−0.8	108.4	386.5	−230.6	−267.1
Foreign exchange losses	—	—	—	—	—	—	—	—	—	—	—	—	—	—	—	—	—	—	—	—	−3.6	−28.3	−130.6	—
Valuation adjustment for exchange rate changes	—	—	—	—	—	—	—	—	—	—	—	—	—	—	—	—	—	—	—	—	—	−31.4	−43.7	14.1

Sources: Data provided by the Albanian authorities; and IMF staff estimates.

currencies. Exports of manufactured goods (mainly textiles) have also become increasingly important in nonconvertible currencies. Exports in convertible currencies were dominated in recent years by crude materials (SITC 2), mainly chrome and nickel. Exports of mineral fuels were important until 1987, but fell sharply thereafter because of production difficulties, whereupon the largest share of these exports was directed toward the nonconvertible currency area, partly because of the resumption of trade with China, and partly because of more favorable prices. On the import side, the major commodity groups in convertible and nonconvertible currencies were manufactured goods and machinery and transport equipment (SITC 6 and 7). Imports of food and live animals (SITC 0) became increasingly important, particularly in convertible currencies after 1987, and by 1990 were the largest convertible currency imports, reflecting the impact of the drought on domestic production. These plus higher imports of manufactured goods explain the increase in total convertible currency imports in 1989–90.

During the 1970s export volumes in both convertible and nonconvertible currencies grew by 17 percent on average annually. However, during 1980–90 total export volumes declined by 6.4 percent on average annually. There was a continued growth in export volumes in convertible currencies (9.7 percent annually), but at a slower pace than in the 1970s, while export volumes in nonconvertible currencies fell by 12 percent annually (Table A26). The volume of exports in nonconvertible currencies fell particularly sharply in 1990, reflecting difficulties in the export markets in East European countries, and the shift of exports to convertible currencies.

Total import volumes continued to expand during the 1980s at only a slightly slower rate than in the 1970s (annual average growth rates of 6.7 and 7.9 percent, respectively), and the growth of import volumes in the 1980s was broadly similar in convertible and nonconvertible currencies. During the 1970s, the growth in import volumes in convertible currencies had far outpaced that in nonconvertible currencies. In 1990, import volumes declined, as much larger imports in convertible currencies were offset by a sharp contraction in nonconvertible currencies.

Albania's average terms of trade generally improved until 1990, when they fell by 27 percent because of much lower export unit values in convertible currencies, especially for chrome ore and nickel, whose prices fell by 30–50 percent. The convertible currency terms of trade improved substantially in the 1970s, declined in the first half of the 1980s, and improved sharply but briefly in

1987 before worsening in 1988–90. The terms of trade in nonconvertible currencies followed an improving trend during the 1980s with higher export and lower import unit values, which compensated for the lower export and higher import volumes in nonconvertible currencies for much of the period.

Before 1978, China was by far Albania's largest trading partner, accounting for two thirds of its total imports and about 20 percent of its exports in 1975. After 1978, trade with China virtually stopped, but began to recover in the mid-1980s. The geographical distribution of trade (Table A28) became more diversified after 1978, shifting toward the industrial countries. In 1990, trade with the CMEA area had fallen to 46 percent and 41 percent of total exports and imports, respectively, from 51 percent and 53 percent, respectively, in 1980. In contrast, the percentage of exports and imports to industrial countries had increased from about 30 percent each in 1980, to 46 percent and 41 percent, respectively, in 1990.

With regard to individual countries, Albania in the early 1980s, increased its exports to Yugoslavia and to several CMEA countries, especially Romania and Czechoslovakia. As this trade was conducted under bilateral payments agreements, there was a commensurate increase in imports from these countries. Trade with Yugoslavia and the CMEA area declined after 1985 as trade with China again became important. In 1990, Albania's exports to several East European countries declined further with the economic restructuring in these countries that reduced the demand for imports and shifted demand toward alternative markets. Trade with industrial countries, especially Italy and Greece, and later Austria and Germany, also increased during the 1980s. In 1990, Albania's main trading partners were Germany (east and west combined), Czechoslovakia, and Italy.

Services and Transfers

Albania's service account was small, reflecting the closed nature of the economy and, until recently, its limited external debt. Receipts consisted mainly of income from transportation, tourism, bank interest, and net reported profits from foreign exchange arbitrage operations, port taxes, and telecommunications; payments consisted mainly of expenditures on transportation, embassies, official travel, port taxes, and telecommunications and, in rubles, interest payments on medium- and long-term debt. Prior to 1991, the service account had been broadly in balance in convertible currencies (but fluctuated from year to year), in small surplus in rubles, and in slight deficit in other nonconvertible currencies.

Capital Account and External Debt

Albania continued to draw on medium- and long-term credits with China until 1978. It continued to utilize short-term trade financing facilities, including letters of credit and countertrade agreements for trade in convertible currencies and balances in clearing accounts for trade under bilateral payments agreements.[47] These facilities were all short term and did not involve a significant, or sustained, net transfer of capital until 1988 when they became a major financing item of the large current account deficits.

Medium- and long-term capital transfers were large and positive until 1978, mainly reflecting loans from China. These credits were all denominated and largely disbursed in rubles. However, some of the credits from China were disbursed in convertible currencies (for repayment in rubles), resulting in a small positive net capital account in convertible currencies in 1969–75. In 1978, Albania unilaterally eliminated rub 981.7 million of external medium- and long-term debt to China, but continued to service rub 34.2 million of other medium- and long-term debt, making the last payment of principal for this debt in 1990 (Table 21). In 1990, Albania contracted its first medium- to long-term bank loan (DM 40 million) to purchase electrical generators. However, these funds were all used to cover foreign exchange market operations and the generators were not purchased.

Short-term external debt has increased substantially since 1988. By June 1991, net short-term debt in nonconvertible currencies had increased to $91 million (at official cross exchange rates), reflecting the balance of payments deficits in non-convertible currencies. Under the various bilateral payments agreements, this debt was to be cleared during 1991 either through shipments of goods, or failing that, payments in convertible currencies. New financing arrangements that would extend the repayment period were under negotiation with some countries, but none had been finalized by end-1991. Net short-term debt in convertible currencies had increased to roughly $384 million by June 1991. In October 1990, the State Bank began delaying payments on its foreign exchange transactions on account of liquidity shortages, and thereafter defaulted on several obligations to about 18 European commercial banks, severely damaging Albania's relations with these banks.

Official Reserves

Official foreign exchange reserves in convertible currencies increased from $16 million in 1970 to $99 million in 1981 (Table 22), when they amounted to the equivalent of 6.8 months of imports in convertible currencies in that year. After 1981, the foreign exchange reserves were drawn down to meet balance of payments deficits in convertible currencies. Foreign exchange reserve management changed substantially in 1988. First, the State Bank became an active participant in the international money market through a newly established foreign exchange dealing operation. At end-1989, the foreign currency placements of the State Bank amounted to $423 million, compared with foreign currency borrowing from banks of $498 million, nearly four times its annual convertible currency exports. Moreover, the State Bank was very active in the spot and forward foreign exchange markets. Second, the State Bank became an active participant in the international gold market, transporting most of its gold holdings to Europe during 1988–90 and using them for trading in the bullion market. By end-1990, it had sold most of its gold reserves.

The State Bank's foreign exchange operations were extensive after 1988. The management of the foreign exchange dealing room of the State Bank operated without any controls. It arranged money market and forward credit lines in excess of $1 billion and drew these down for currency speculation and funding. During 1988–90, a very large speculative position was taken on the possibility of a depreciation in the deutsche mark. However, the exchange rate of the deutsche mark against the U.S. dollar appreciated by 25 percent. This resulted in foreign exchange losses amounting to about $163 million (10 percent of GDP). Foreign exchange and international money market activities were curtailed during 1990 and 1991 with the cutback in credit lines, the subsequent emergence of arrears on transactions with commercial banks, and the exhaustion of foreign exchange reserves. By end-June 1991 usable foreign exchange reserves had fallen to $15 million, less than two weeks of total imports.

The net short-term asset position in nonconvertible currencies fell in the early 1980s and became negative in 1987. At end-April 1991, net short-term foreign liabilities in rubles amounted to rub 68 million, and in other nonconvertible currencies to $48 million. Under the bilateral payments agreements, these balances were expected to be cleared by end-1991.

---

[47]These agreements specified the "swing" credit limits, above which balances in the accounts had to be settled by a time and method specified therein. Balances in accounts denominated in rubles were settled through the transfer of goods; whereas balances in accounts denominated in other nonconvertible currencies were settled in goods, or failing this, in convertible currencies. Balances outstanding in ruble clearing accounts in 1991 are to be settled in convertible currencies.

Table 21. External Debt in Convertible and Nonconvertible Currencies
(In millions of U.S. dollars unless otherwise stated; end of period)

	1970	1975	1980	1981	1982	1983	1984	1985	1986	1987	1988	1989	1990	June 1991 Estimate
Debt in convertible currencies														
Medium- and long-term	—	—	—	—	—	—	—	—	—	—	—	—	29.1	23.1
Short-term (net)[1]	—	—	—	—	—	—	—	—	—	—	—	74.4	312.9	383.6
Total, convertible currencies	—	—	—	—	—	—	—	—	—	—	—	74.4	342.0	406.7
Debt in nonconvertible currencies														
Medium- and long-term (rubles)	463.4	813.9	21.4[2]	18.8	16.1	14.1	12.0	10.0	8.0	5.9	3.9	2.0	—	—
Short-term (net)	13.6	−21.2	−16.3	−32.0	−20.4	−5.0	−9.6	−3.4	−5.7	16.8	53.2	44.5	80.3	90.7
Total[3]	543.2	1,138.1	16.1[2]	−7.0	1.1	13.8	6.5	9.9	2.2	22.8	57.1	46.4	80.3	90.7
Total convertible and nonconvertible currencies[3]	543.2	1,138.1	16.1[2]	−7.0	1.1	13.8	6.5	9.9	2.2	22.8	57.1	120.8	422.3	497.4
Memorandum item:														
Debt in convertible currencies in percent of annual exports in convertible currencies	—	—	—	—	—	—	—	—	—	—	—	56.1	278.0	492.4

Sources: State Bank of Albania; and IMF staff estimates.

[1] Includes short-term contractual debt to governments and banks, arrears on spot and money market transactions, letters of credit, overdue interest, and an estimate of unmatured letters of credit, and is net of the State Bank of Albania's deposits in foreign currency.

[2] In 1978 Albania eliminated claims on and liabilities to China. The amount of external debt eliminated was rub 981.7 million ($1,435.2 million at the then official cross exchange rate).

[3] Debt in rubles converted using official cross exchange rates.

Table 22. Official External Reserves and Other Foreign Assets
(In millions of U.S. dollars; end of period)

	1970	1975	1980	1981	1982	1983	1984	1985	1986	1987	1988	1989	1990	June 1991 Estimate
Official external reserves	23.6	59.7	82.6	108.8	95.3	54.0	42.0	24.4	23.0	34.7	165.3	429.5	223.2	16.6
Gold[1]	8.0	8.4	9.6	9.9	10.0	10.3	10.5	10.7	10.8	10.9	8.5	6.2	1.6	1.9
Foreign exchange	15.6	51.3	73.0	98.9	85.3	43.8	31.6	13.8	12.3	23.8	156.8	423.3	221.6	14.7
Short-term foreign liabilities in convertible currencies held by State Bank of Albania	—	—	2.0	3.7	2.0	2.4	2.6	3.3	2.0	2.7	111.2	497.7	473.0	331.8
Deposits	—	—	2.0	3.7	2.0	2.4	2.6	3.3	2.0	2.7	111.2	497.7	267.1	—
Arrears	—	—	—	—	—	—	—	—	—	—	—	—	206.0	331.8
Net international reserves														
Gold at $42.22 an ounce	23.6	59.7	80.6	105.0	93.3	51.6	39.4	21.1	21.1	32.0	54.2	-68.2	-249.8	-315.2
Gold at current market price	22.4	83.4	210.9	202.6	172.7	144.6	118.5	90.8	104.3	136.6	133.6	-18.5	-236.9	-301.3
Foreign assets in nonconvertible currencies (net) Held by State Bank of Albania														
Total	-13.6	21.2	16.3	47.8	20.4	5.0	9.6	3.4	5.7	-16.8	-53.2	-44.5	-80.3	-90.7
Rubles	-10.7	3.0	12.0	20.1	24.7	8.2	13.1	9.7	11.3	-4.1	-27.1	-12.5	-41.2	-54.0
Clearing dollars	-2.9	18.2	4.3	20.7	-4.3	-3.2	-3.5	-9.5	-5.6	-12.8	-26.1	-32.0	-39.0	-47.5
Memorandum item:														
Gold in ounces	188,900	199,200	227,600	233,500	238,000	243,700	248,400	253,100	255,600	258,800	201,391	146,516	37,800	45,217

Sources: State Bank of Albania; and IMF staff estimates.

[1] Valued at $42.22 an ounce.

IV Political and Economic Developments in 1991

The critical condition of Albania's economy deteriorated further in 1991. As existing institutional structures collapsed, inappropriate financial policies and social unrest exacerbated macroeconomic imbalances and impaired output growth.

During 1991 three governments came to power. After the first free elections in 45 years, the Party of Labor (later renamed the Socialist Party) supported by rural votes formed a government in April. Following large-scale strikes and protracted unrest, in early June a new coalition government of "national stability" (comprising members of all parties, including the Socialist and the Democratic Party) was formed. Members of the Democratic Party held most of the key economic positions and were primarily responsible for initiating new economic policies and introducing legislation on economic reforms. However, in early December, the Democratic Party members of the coalition government resigned, accusing the Socialist Party of stalling legislation on political and economic reform. A new caretaker government was then formed, with technocrats, independent of party affiliations, assuming most ministerial positions. New general elections were held in late March 1992, with the Democratic Party defeating its closest rival, the Socialist Party, by a large margin, and winning the elections by a clear majority.

The data on economic developments in 1991 are highly tentative, as the reporting system was adversely affected by the breakdown in administration and the rapid emergence of unrecorded parallel market transactions. Gross output is officially estimated to have declined by about 24 percent in agriculture and 37 percent in industry. Aggregate supply constraints that affected all sectors of the economy were largely reflected in food shortages, production stoppages, and the inability to import essential inputs. In contrast, domestic demand continued to increase sharply, stimulated by large nominal wage increases and a loss of control in the fiscal and monetary areas.

Food shortages became widespread. Crop production is estimated to have dropped by more than 35 percent, with maize and wheat registering the worst declines. The "spontaneous privatization" that resulted in the dismantling of agricultural cooperatives (which owned 75–80 percent of the arable land during the 1980s), and the uncertainty about ownership rights as well as continuing shortages in fertilizers, seeds, pesticides, insecticides, and spare parts for machinery and equipment sharply constrained farming activities. As a result, large areas of field crops were not sown, inducing substantial declines in crop yields. Livestock production in 1991 declined marginally, by about 7 percent compared with 1990, since live animals were distributed relatively early to cooperative members.

In addition to low production, the availability of food was further impeded by the breakdown of the state distribution and marketing system. The role of the *grumbullims*, the state distribution entities, diminished considerably, as farmers preferred to sell their products in emerging free markets, and the services rendered by the machine and tractor stations deteriorated sharply. Hence, in 1991, free agricultural markets for inputs and output did not fully develop, and the organized system through which the former cooperative members bought inputs and sold their products collapsed. The severe inadequacy of transport aggravated the situation.

Following attempts by nearly 40,000 Albanians to flee to Italy during 1991, and in response to the Albanian Government's request for food aid, the Group of Twenty-Four (principally Italy) responded by committing over $200 million in food and commodity aid, of which a substantial sum has already been disbursed by Italy.

With social unrest persisting and essential inputs unavailable, gross industrial output in 1991 is estimated to have reached roughly 60 percent of the previous year's level. Production, in food, light industry, and some areas of heavy industry (cement, machinery and equipment, and spare parts) sharply declined, with the result that state shops were unable to meet the demands for nonfood items as well. In fact, by the third quarter of 1991, there was increasing evidence of private markets supplying goods from neighboring Greece, Yugoslavia, and Italy.

Most state enterprises had either shut down or were operating at very low capacity by end-1991. Consequently, about 115,000–130,000 employees were inactive, although the wage policy in force ensured that they continued to receive 80 percent of their wages. Moreover, as a result of political pressures, wages and salaries of all state employees (including those not working) were arbitrarily increased by over 50 percent in 1991. Thus, substantive across-the-board wage increases had actually *preceded* wide-ranging price liberalization measures. These wage increases are expected to result in a nearly 25 percent increase in money incomes in 1991 whereas expenditures will decline by 15 percent owing to acute shortages in goods and services. The number of registered unemployed also increased, from 33,200 at end-1990 to 78,500 at end-1991.

At the root of Albania's financial imbalances during 1991 was the dramatic worsening in its fiscal position, arising primarily from price and enterprise subsidies, wage increases, and the collapse of an outdated and ineffective revenue mobilization mechanism. The 1991 budget deficit before grants was about 34 percent of GDP on a commitment basis.

The accommodation of excess demand by a passive monetary policy contributed to a liquidity overhang, fueling inflationary expectations, particularly in the first half of the year when most prices were still controlled. In 1991 the velocity of broad money declined by 40 percent. Most of the growth in money supply was reflected in cash held by the public, as interest rates, although marginally raised in the fourth quarter, continued to be fixed at very low levels, and transaction costs associated with withdrawing and depositing cash remained high. Consequently, the 12-month rate of growth of currency in circulation accelerated to about 170 percent by the end of 1991. Household liquidity increased by about 140 percent, reaching a level equivalent to about 47 percent of GDP.

Although official prices continued to be largely controlled, increases in aggregate demand had put an upward pressure on prices. After remaining virtually fixed for several decades, some consumer prices were officially liberalized in November 1991 (excluding a basket of commodities with a weight of 40 percent, which remained controlled throughout 1991 and the first half of 1992) and were roughly estimated to have increased on a 12-month basis by 104 percent by December 1991. The impact of partial price liberalization in November 1991 led to a further acceleration of inflation in early 1992.

As a cumulative result of the disruptions in the production and distribution systems, continued controls on prices and the exchange system, and the lax financial policies, the worsening external position was inevitable. Exports fell rapidly, by more than 40 percent, constraining the country's ability to import essentials; a cutback was particularly evident in the areas of raw materials, machinery, spare parts, and intermediate inputs, as available foreign exchange was used primarily to import food. Moreover, inappropriate external reserve management led to a virtual exhaustion of foreign reserves and to the accumulation of sizable arrears on external payments. With the deterioration of financial imbalances and the rise in open inflation, the economy became increasingly "dollarized."

During 1991, Albania portrayed a grim picture of poverty and economic decline in Europe. Even though it was trying to shed its legacy of economic and political isolation, its starting conditions and reform prospects were daunting. The administrative system had virtually collapsed and social unrest and crime were on the rise. Despite its poor economic performance and against many obstacles, the authorities nevertheless made efforts in effecting liberalization measures, particularly those relating to structural reforms in the agricultural sector. The progress made in Albania's economic reform program is examined in the following section.

V Toward Economic Reform

Practically no economic reforms were introduced in Albania before 1990. In 1985, after decades of centralist rule, the Government started, albeit slowly, to move away from adherence to the principle of self-reliance. But only by the middle of 1990, in response to popular unrest, did the Albanian authorities acknowledge that the system of central planning had led to the accumulation of serious imbalances. Within the framework of the "new economic mechanism" adopted at that time, some limited measures were introduced, aimed at integrating Albania into the world economy and at promoting a gradual transition from central planning to a market-oriented system.

The Socialist Government formed after the March 1991 elections and the "national stability" coalition that took office in June 1991 opted for a gradualist approach to economic reform. Numerous reform initiatives were prepared, and some were discussed by Parliament. However, in spite of important breakthroughs, particularly in the privatization of agricultural activities, financial autonomy of state enterprises, and price determination, the pace of reform remained slow, and an uncoordinated, piecemeal approach prevailed in the design of the reform measures. Such measures were also inadequately publicized and slowly implemented by a weak economic administration. In the event, conflicts and delays in the reform process led to increasing dissent among the coalition parties, which culminated in a new government crisis in December 1991 and in the decision to move the general elections forward to March 1992.

Major and fundamental issues will have to be resolved by the authorities in their attempt to promote the transition to a market-oriented economy. Economic reforms have to be integrated into a comprehensive package that addresses the urgent need to stabilize the economy and at the same time promotes the removal of remaining restrictions. At the macroeconomic level, it is imperative to develop instruments and institutions to regain fiscal and monetary control and to introduce a market-based exchange rate system supported by tight financial and wage policies. At the microeconomic level, the authorities face the challenge of correcting a severe lack of financial discipline in the management of state enterprises, the persistent labor market rigidities, and the presence of little competition and limited private sector activities in most sectors of the economy.

External Sector Reforms

External sector reforms have focused on removing legal impediments to foreign credit and foreign investment and on partially liberalizing foreign trade and exchange restrictions.

In July 1990, two decrees (Decree No. 7406 "On the protection of foreign investments in the People's Socialist Republic of Albania" and Decree No. 7407 "On the economic activity of enterprises with participation of foreign capital in the People's Socialist Republic of Albania") were approved by the Albanian Parliament, which lifted the constitutional ban on foreign borrowing introduced in 1976.[48] The decrees allowed foreign direct investment, established legal protection against arbitrary expropriation and nationalization, and permitted joint ventures of foreign firms with Albanian enterprises and the remittance of profits abroad.[49] Bilateral investment treaties were subsequently signed with various partner countries, and in August 1991 a Foreign Investment Agency was established under the Ministry of Foreign Economic Relations and made responsible for investment promotion and review of investment proposals.

In August 1990, Albania began liberalizing its

---

[48]The entire 1976 Constitution was subsequently abrogated on April 29, 1991, and pending the adoption of a new constitution, which is currently being drafted, Parliament (elected in March 1991) adopted Law No. 7491, entitled "Principal Constitutional Provisions," which confirmed the liberalization measures introduced in these decrees.

[49]Tax incentives for the formation of joint ventures with foreign capital investment included reduced profit tax rates for a period of two years.

trade and exchange system. Until then, foreign trade had been conducted exclusively through a small number of foreign trade monopolies under government control. After August 1990, all state enterprises were authorized to conduct foreign trade operations directly. In April 1991, following the Council of Ministers' decision on privatization, the state monopoly on foreign trade ended, allowing private enterprises and individuals to conduct international trade operations independently. This gradual dismantling of the state monopoly on foreign trade was accompanied by the introduction (in December 1990) of a system of import and export licensing and limited foreign exchange retention rights, extended in April 1991 to export earnings of private enterprises. Since August 1991, exports and imports have been liberalized, except for a list of commodities requiring a specific license issued by the Ministry of Foreign Economic Relations, and except for a prohibition on the export of food items owing to widespread shortages. Since January 1991, all trade has been conducted in convertible currencies, all the bilateral payments agreements have been denominated in U.S. dollars, and the exchange rates for commercial and noncommercial transactions are no longer differentiated. Since September 1991, the official exchange rate has been pegged to the European currency unit (ECU) (at the rate of leks 30 = ECU 1), although in practice a peg to the U.S dollar prevailed at the adjusted rate of leks 25 = $1 (up from leks 10 = $1 set at the beginning of 1991). With the loss of control by the Government over foreign exchange surrender requirements and the almost complete depletion of foreign exchange reserves, in early 1992 the official rate was further devalued to leks 50 = $1. Parallel market transactions in foreign exchange took place in increasing volume, with the market-determined exchange rate for the U.S. dollar rising from leks 40–43 in early November 1991 to leks 78–81 in February 1992.

Domestic Economy Reforms

Reforms of the domestic economy were aimed at modifying the legal and institutional framework regulating economic activities, allowing private initiatives, providing limited financial support for private sector development, and increasing the financial autonomy of state enterprises in relation to the budget. However, because price controls remained in place for most commodities until end-October 1991, the dismantling of the centralized system of resource allocation was not accompanied by the simultaneous introduction of clear market incentives. The protracted lack of price flexibility, the breakdown of the institutional

framework for management, the work disincentives resulting from the continued payment of 80 percent of wages to idle workers, and the acute shortages of raw materials inhibited the supply response of the economy and contributed to aggravating financial imbalances.

Legal and institutional reforms considerably diminished the role of central planning and began to address the issue of ownership rights. In March–April 1991, the Government decided to abandon the traditional five-year plan and replace it by a set of annual indicative targets for 1991 under an "operational plan." These indicative targets were set against the background of a rapid erosion of work discipline experienced since 1990 throughout the country. Also since March–April 1991, by Decree No. 7476 "On permission and protection of private ownership and private activities,"[50] and through preliminary constitutional provisions approved by Parliament, private ownership of all types of property (except land initially)[51] has been permitted and granted equal legal protection in relation to other forms of ownership, whether public, mixed, or joint.

Privatization was envisaged initially as consisting of private entry into small-scale industries, trade, and services. At the same time, splitting larger enterprises into smaller units was to proceed, and subsequently large-scale enterprises were to be sold to the public. (Decision No. 138 "On development of private activity," approved by Parliament on April 3, 1991, required the Government to identify the sectors and the specific state enterprises to be privatized, but in practice, this process is still under way.) In legislation and decisions approved in August 1991, privatization was again addressed.[52] Under the auspices of the newly created Preparatory Commission for the Process of Privatization (PCPP) and the National Privatization Agency (NPA), state enterprises were either to be auctioned, sold through shares, freely distributed through vouchers or shares (up to 30 percent of the enterprise value), or a combination thereof. The PCPP would be responsible for valuing state assets and state enterprises, and the NPA for intermediating between the state and the buyers and for effecting the final sale of state

---

[50]The protection of private property, private economic activities, and foreign investment was confirmed in legislation adopted in August 1991.

[51]Decree No. 7476 envisaged land use as remaining regulated by leasing contracts under state ownership. Private use and ownership of land has in principle been permitted by Law No. 7501 of July 1991, but transfer of land remains restricted.

[52]The Law on Privatization approved by Parliament on August 15, 1991, and decisions of the Council of Ministers Nos. 300 (August 28, 1991) and 307 (August 29, 1991).

enterprises. The sale of state assets typically would proceed by giving the first option to buy to the enterprise employees, then by auctioning the property to all Albanian citizens, and finally, for unsold properties, by opening the auction to foreign individuals and companies. The proceeds were to be transferred to the state budget.

Nonagricultural private sector activities have increased, but to a limited extent. As of early 1992, only the privatization of small retail shops and other commercial services had progressed substantially, while only about 20 percent of state enterprises in the food industry were privatized.[53] A number of new small-scale private trading activities were established throughout the country, giving rise to a rapid development of parallel markets. Financial support for the creation of private initiatives was undertaken in January 1991 through a specific medium-term credit program (involving a maximum ceiling of leks 40,000 for each investment project), but loans extended under this program remained throughout 1991 an insignificant proportion of total domestic credit.

Reforms proceeded more rapidly in the agricultural sector, and in the trade of agricultural products. Since mid-1990, legal parallel markets have been allowed for agricultural produce of private plots, which had previously been cultivated by cooperative members for self-consumption. Prices in these markets have been market determined, and the volume of transactions has risen first as a result of the increase in the size of private plots for cooperative members, and, after the first quarter of 1991, through the spontaneous breaking up of agricultural cooperatives. The criteria for the distribution of land and other property of cooperatives (which owned about 75–80 percent of arable land) were set by the Council of Ministers in August 1991, after a distribution of part of the livestock among cooperative members. As of mid-1992, about 70–75 percent of arable land previously controlled by cooperatives had been freely distributed to private occupants. Land could be transferred to descendants, but legislation approved in July 1991 prohibited its sale. In addition, severe inadequacies in the transportation, distribution, and marketing facilities for agricultural products continued to hamper the development of farming activities. The reform of state farms had yet to be initiated as of mid-1992.

After the middle of 1990, a number of reforms were introduced to increase the financial autonomy of state enterprises.[54] In essence, these measures influenced the financial flows between state enterprises and the state budget, in an attempt to make enterprises responsible for their investment decisions. Specifically, the proportion of an enterprise's retained profits increased from less than 10 percent to 90 percent, while investments, completely financed by the budget before the reform, were to be financed by the enterprise's own funds and by bank credit. Financial dependence on the state budget still applies for large investment projects, such as irrigation infrastructure in agriculture and hydroelectric power plants, as well as for research activities. Losses once fully covered by the budget were to be financed by bank credit in the first year, and their continuation for a second year would lead, in principle, to the enterprise's bankruptcy. (No bankruptcy laws had been approved by mid-1992.) In practice, however, bank credit continued to be unconditionally extended to insolvent state enterprises. In addition, the decentralization of production, pricing, and wage setting decisions were legally addressed only in the last quarter of 1991. The bill on state enterprises published in October 1991 sanctioned in principle their autonomy regarding structure of production, level of work force employed, the setting of wages and prices, and the freedom to produce on a contractual basis. However, important restrictions remained. The state continued to have the right to place orders up to two thirds of the productive capacity, and up to 100 percent in specific sectors. Employment decisions remained subject to the control of branch ministries or local authorities. Pricing decisions were administratively restricted, in spite of partial price liberalization measures introduced in November 1991. A significant range of commodities remained under price controls, but implementation was limited by the weakening of the administrative structures in 1991 and early 1992.[55]

Although as of mid-1992 major steps still needed to be taken by the Albanian authorities for the stabilization and structural reform of the economy, the clear electoral victory of the political party most committed to reform should accelerate the reform process.

---

[53]The monitoring of privatization remains disorganized, however, and little control is exercised over the transfer of private proceeds to the budget.

[54]The reforms of state enterprises in industry initiated in July 1990 were also applicable to state farms and to state enterprises in the construction and internal trade sectors.

[55]Commodities remaining under price control included (a) 12 food items and 14 nonfood items whose retail prices were administratively set by the Council of Ministers; (b) 12 food items and 5 nonfood industrial items whose wholesale prices remained administratively set by the Council of Ministers; and (c) 10 nonfood industrial items whose wholesale prices were set by the Ministry of Finance.

Bibliography

Biberaj, Elez, *Albania: A Socialist Maverick* (Boulder, Colorado: Westview Press, 1990).

———, "Albania After Hoxha: Dilemmas of Change," *Problems of Communism,* Vol. 34 (November/December 1985), pp. 32–47.

Freedman, Robert Owen, *Economic Warfare in the Communist Bloc: A Study of Soviet Economic Pressure Against Yugoslavia, Albania, and Communist China* (New York: Praeger, 1970).

Gianaris, Nicholas V., *The Economies of the Balkan Countries: Albania, Bulgaria, Greece, Romania, Turkey, and Yugoslavia* (New York: Praeger, 1982).

Great Britain, Department of Trade and Industry, *Albania: A Country Profile,* Prepared by the Department of Trade and Industry (1985).

———, Economist Intelligence Unit, *Country Report: Albania* (London: Economist Intelligence Unit Ltd., 1980–present).

Keefe, Eugene K., and The American University, *Albania: A Country Study* (Washington: Government Printing Office, 1982).

Lear, Aaron E., *Albania* (Edgemont, Pennsylvania: Chelsea House, 1987).

Logoreci, Anton, *The Albanians: Europe's Forgotten Survivors* (Boulder, Colorado: Westview Press, 1977).

Pano, Nicholas C., *The People's Republic of Albania* (Baltimore: Johns Hopkins Press, 1968).

Pipa, Arshi, *Albanian Stalinism: Ideo-political Aspects,* East European Monographs, No. 287 (Boulder, Colorado: East European Monographs, 1990).

Prifti, Peter R., *Socialist Albania Since 1944: Domestic and Foreign Developments* (Cambridge, Massachusetts: MIT Press, 1978).

Sandstrom, Per, and Sjoberg, Orjan, "Albanian Economic Performance: Stagnation in the 1980s," *Soviet Studies,* Vol. 43, No. 5 (1991), pp. 931–47.

Schnytzer, Adi, *Stalinist Economic Strategy in Practice: The Case of Albania* (New York: Oxford University Press, 1982).

Sjoberg, Orjan, *Rural Change and Development in Albania* (Boulder, Colorado: Westview Press, 1991).

Appendix: Albanian Statistics

Table A1. Conversion from MPS to SNA Accounts—Summary Table—in Current Prices, 1980–89[1]

A. = Material Product Balances (MPS) aggregates B. = United Nations System of National Accounts (SNA) aggregates	1980	1981	1982	1983	1984	1985	1986	1987	1988	1989
A. MPS net material product	12,862	13,264	13,625	13,697	13,300	13,602	14,013	13,699	13,631	15,223
plus: Consumption of fixed capital in material and nonmaterial spheres	1,682	1,736	1,801	1,903	1,982	2,052	2,100	2,146	2,089	2,198
plus: Value added in nonmaterial services	1,346	1,436	1,496	1,508	1,610	1,601	1,668	1,809	1,686	1,694
minus: Expenditures for material goods and services during business trips	41	43	47	49	52	55	43	56	58	60
minus: Nonmaterial services used in material sphere	311	320	331	334	330	337	348	345	340	374
equals:										
B. SNA gross domestic product	15,538	16,073	16,544	16,725	16,510	16,863	17,390	17,253	17,008	18,681

Source: State Planning Commission.
[1] Preliminary estimates.

Table A2. Agricultural Production, 1980–90
(In millions of leks at constant 1986 prices)

	1989	1980	1981	1982	1983	1984	1985	1986	1987	1988	1989	1990
	(Share in total agri-cultural production)											
Total gross agricultural production	100.0	6,987	7,245	7,533	8,240	7,785	8,081	8,402	8,441	7,921	8,772	8,120
Crop production	54.7	3,946	4,278	4,562	4,992	4,597	4,837	5,080	4,995	4,423	4,795	4,071
Grains	15.7	1,146	1,124	1,206	1,347	1,229	1,363	1,303	1,341	1,440	1,373	1,381
Maize	5.9	596	653	717	751	671	577	748	633	485	519	470
Rice	0.3	39	44	38	39	37	39	35	34	28	27	22
Potatoes	1.2	109	131	111	148	115	94	121	99	66	104	75
Vegetables	7.4	598	618	648	668	618	610	627	642	525	649	639
Kidney beans	1.1	45	60	40	81	36	66	101	75	74	100	68
Tobacco	2.7	211	283	280	251	294	259	341	355	191	238	224
Sunflower seeds	1.1	116	126	131	215	132	146	132	97	71	96	53
Cotton	1.1	96	124	125	94	118	162	164	144	87	100	72
Sugar beets	0.9	83	91	96	96	75	69	58	58	38	79	49
Other[1]	17.2	907	1,024	1,170	1,302	1,272	1,452	1,450	1,517	1,418	1,510	1,018
Fruits and olives	6.9	548	589	611	691	556	578	539	572	537	602	516
Apples, pears, peaches, figs	1.7	129	174	157	178	141	118	140	122	117	150	121
Grapes	1.8	132	141	160	161	158	163	127	155	150	158	131
Olives	0.8	58	51	38	108	17	72	38	81	50	66	32
Citrus fruits	0.5	30	26	35	39	38	37	39	28	38	42	42
Others[2]	2.1	199	197	221	205	202	188	195	186	182	186	190
Livestock	32.0	2,180	2,079	2,067	2,234	2,304	2,323	2,456	2,571	2,616	2,807	2,963
Meat	9.8	598	707	609	616	702	818	877	925	874	862	890
Cattle	3.8	275	350	273	267	291	328	380	402	348	336	346
Pigs	2.3	137	146	144	134	167	180	195	191	183	198	206
Sheep and goats	2.7	140	162	135	146	147	207	201	231	247	236	245
Poultry	1.0	46	49	57	69	97	103	101	101	96	92	93
Milk	13.6	892	806	778	845	890	907	933	991	1,066	1,195	1,138
Eggs	2.7	132	126	143	159	175	177	189	210	212	240	252
Others[3]	5.8	558	440	537	614	537	421	457	445	464	510	683
Forestry and related activities	6.5	313	299	293	323	328	343	327	303	345	568	570
Social product[4]	100.0	7,357	7,630	7,940	8,635	8,195	8,498	8,828	8,878	8,376	9,215	8,540
Material inputs	46.6	3,266	3,338	3,626	3,970	3,796	3,853	4,060	4,328	4,080	4,296	4,251
Net material product	53.4	4,091	4,292	4,314	4,665	4,399	4,645	4,768	4,550	4,296	4,919	4,289

Source: State Planning Commission.
[1]Includes planting of new crops.
[2]Includes planting of new orchards.
[3]Includes production of wool, silk, organic fertilizer.
[4]The difference between social product and gross agricultural production is accounted for by turnover taxes, irrigation, and production from personal plots.

Table A3. Industrial Production, 1980–90
(In millions of leks at 1986 constant prices)

	1980	1981	1982	1983	1984	1985	1986	1987	1988	1989	1990
Energy											
Electricity	486	557	524	432	480	439	594	543	527	543	463
Oil	1,214	1,191	1,115	880	879	837	880	842	844	851	804
Mining											
Coal	182	197	212	229	248	257	263	263	274	276	261
Chromium	230	250	265	257	278	256	307	281	326	340	265
Copper	852	935	1,042	1,071	1,234	1,162	1,304	1,370	1,461	1,525	1,134
Iron-nickel	397	511	474	602	570	512	486	528	622	671	521
Manufacturing											
Chemical and rubber	625	678	799	770	772	841	888	937	965	1,017	857
Building material	1,045	1,071	1,111	1,106	1,123	985	1,023	1,008	983	996	879
Wood processing	655	669	695	712	723	736	758	729	708	742	662
Paper	123	133	136	134	133	144	161	153	144	165	152
Machinery and equipment	350	372	425	468	503	465	495	513	496	486	369
Spare parts	327	350	374	399	404	407	466	485	493	513	482
Electrotechnical and											
metalworks	990	1,129	1,234	1,283	1,337	1,356	1,367	1,396	1,409	1,490	1,492
Glass and ceramics	118	132	140	132	146	131	139	125	139	152	142
Other minerals	86	105	107	110	124	109	109	110	108	115	116
Textiles	700	736	729	771	701	778	793	778	778	795	713
Clothing	812	829	887	914	878	922	866	883	956	1,146	1,318
Leather processing	265	279	298	302	319	302	317	350	385	412	432
Other light industry	288	389	431	455	420	484	641	569	570	616	596
Tobacco products	145	150	165	155	165	158	171	164	163	195	158
Fishery	38	42	52	45	48	61	58	66	74	66	78
Flour, bread	1,348	1,390	1,400	1,435	1,499	1,543	1,543	1,608	1,635	1,676	1,720
Other food and											
beverages	2,712	2,820	2,920	2,965	3,069	2,976	3,031	3,153	3,144	3,273	3,089
Print	105	111	113	114	112	116	121	123	120	130	124
Other	52	59	76	110	97	105	110	164	173	179	169
Total gross output	14,145	15,085	15,724	15,851	16,262	16,082	16,891	17,141	17,497	18,370	16,996
Capital goods	9,024	9,705	10,014	10,015	10,387	10,224	10,951	10,956	11,177	11,574	10,237
Consumer goods	5,121	5,380	5,710	5,836	5,875	5,858	5,940	6,185	6,320	6,796	6,759
Social production[1]	17,101	18,096	18,979	19,031	19,304	19,210	20,128	20,491	20,821	21,695	21,272
Material inputs	11,877	12,633	13,264	13,354	13,704	13,573	13,932	14,215	14,511	14,873	15,185
Net material production	5,224	5,463	5,715	5,677	5,600	5,637	6,196	6,276	6,310	6,822	6,087
Turnover taxes	2,956	3,011	3,255	3,180	3,042	3,128	3,237	3,350	3,324	3,325	4,276

Source: State Planning Commission.
[1] Turnover taxes account for the difference between gross output and social production.

Table A4. Output of Selected Industrial Products, 1950–June 1991

Product	Unit	1950	1960	1970	1980	1985	1986	1987	1988	1989	1990	Jan.–June 1990	Jan.–June 1991
Crude oil	000 tons	132	728	1,487	1,388	1,188	1,205	1,182	1,167	1,128	1,067	539	453
Natural gas	m. m3	—	43	98	696	204	263	236	186	233	243	130	74
Benzine	000 tons	5	54	76	199	131	109	124	109	91	81	43	41
Petroleum	000 tons	3	2	15	44	55	55	56	60	61	56	24	33
Electric power	m. Kwh	21	194	952	3,717	3,147	5,106	4,395	3,984	4,123	3,198	1,715	1,764
Lignite	000 tons	41	291	606	1,418	2,100	2,167	2,134	2,184	2,193	2,071	1,132	710
Metallurgical coke	000 tons	—	—	—	173	250	238	260	291	290	230	119	83
Chromium ore	000 tons	52	289	466	1,004	1,111	1,159	1,075	1,109	1,200	1,011	568	360
Chromium concentrate	000 tons	—	—	—	117	171	186	164	160	173	157	84	56
Ferrochrome	000 tons	—	—	—	12	12	26	26	39	39	24	15	17
Copper ore	000 tons	14	82	339	769	989	1,012	1,166	1,087	1,136	931	519	388
Copper wire	000 tons	—	—	3	6	9	11	11	12	12	9	5	2
Iron/nickel ore	000 tons	—	255	401	597	905	829	972	1,067	1,179	931	529	341
Rolled steel	000 tons	—	—	33	96	107	93	101	97	93	65	36	9
Molded steel	000 tons	—	—	—	134	126	117	127	114	112	79	43	11
Phosphatic fertilizer	000 tons	—	—	111	150	157	168	175	165	165	142	80	30
Ammonium nitrate	000 tons	—	—	76	109	95	111	103	96	109	93	48	13
Urea	000 tons	—	—	—	88	78	93	74	77	92	90	50	14
Sulfuric acid	000 tons	—	—	46	72	73	86	80	81	82	68	37	14
Caustic soda	000 tons	—	—	13	25	29	29	31	31	33	33	16	7
Soda ash	000 tons	—	—	11	23	22	22	21	22	27	23	13	3
Machinery and equipment	m. leks	—	2	107	350	465	495	513	496	486	369	197	107
Spare parts	m. leks	—	16	97	327	407	466	485	493	513	482	222	121
Cement	000 tons	16	73	345	826	642	710	709	746	754	645	346	193
Bricks and tiles	m. pieces	18	165	240	295	291	312	313	319	327	308	157	106
Sawn timber	000 m3	51	170	191	205	194	196	177	171	173	156	83	36
Firewood	000 tons	. . .	1,008	969	1,201	1,381	1,384	1,290	1,243	1,318	1,182	664	489
Veneer	000 m3	—	6	10	7	7	7	7	6	8	6	. . .	. . .
Furniture	m. leks	5	32	64	86	112	125	129	131	145	133	66	32
Printing/writing paper	ton	—	—	3,351	7,619	7,659	8,450	7,840	6,739	8,145	7,546	4,105	1,844
Packing paper	ton	—	—	3,342	7,130	6,638	8,611	8,059	7,503	8,477	6,852	3,520	1,350
Cotton clothes	m. ms	1	22	44	49	46	46	41	38	38	33	18	6
Fabrics	m. ms	1	4	10	13	12	13	12	11	12	9	4	2
Knitwear	000 pieces	—	1	4	10	11	11	12	12	11	10	7	3
Footwear	000 pair	291	1,342	3,680	4,735	4,800	5,376	5,314	5,396	6,103	5,990	3,092	1,386
Lamps	000 pieces	—	—	742	4,315	4,928	5,093	4,798	5,042	5,560	4,344	. . .	. . .
TV sets	000 pieces	—	—	1	21	21	22	20	17	23	18	8	4
Radio sets	000 pieces	—	—	6	8	16	17	25	25	30	26	12	9
Plastic products	m. leks	—	—	9	94	126	128	119	125	175	132	. . .	. . .
Flour	000 tons	28	125	190	278	311	317	332	338	343	352	. . .	. . .
Bread	000 tons	51	138	223	300	330	341	352	358	371	378	. . .	. . .
Sugar	000 tons	1	13	15	33	23	21	18	12	23	15	. . .	. . .
Edible oils	000 tons	1	3	9	20	19	18	19	14	15	10	. . .	. . .
Olive oil	ton	—	—	1,571	4,825	2,948	2,164	2,854	3,594	3,055	1,246	. . .	. . .
Industrial oils	ton	500	1,686	2,148	5,494	4,203	4,608	4,685	4,373	3,525	2,226	. . .	. . .
Canned fish	ton	—	352	623	1,047	1,253	1,281	1,291	1,441	1,042	1,070	. . .	. . .
Cheese	000 tons	1	2	6	10	13	13	13	14	14	11	7	2
Macaroni	000 tons	3	8	14	24	27	27	28	30	30	26	14	12
Rice	ton	655	2,207	7,825	7,862	7,423	6,373	6,185	5,962	4,299	3,528	. . .	. . .
Preserves and compotes	ton	—	717	3,510	4,160	4,678	5,098	5,562	6,410	7,539	5,645	. . .	. . .
Beer	000 hl	21	69	117	150	199	229	240	237	228	187	100	51
Cigarettes	m. pieces	733	3,436	3,905	4,950	5,348	5,624	5,467	5,310	6,184	4,947	2,979	1,095
Soaps and detergents	000 tons	1	4	9	15	18	21	25	22	25	21	12	5

Source: State Planning Commission.

Table A5. Summary Energy Balance, 1975–90
(In thousand tons of oil equivalent)

Item	1975	1980	1981	1982	1983	1984	1985	1986	1987	1988	1989	1990
Total domestic sources	2,741	2,935	3,045	3,054	2,485	2,505	2,482	2,740	2,644	2,549	2,570	2,418
Total imports	55	124	186	237	228	200	226	203	237	294	392	314
From CMEA	12	16	19	15	104	55	52	80	111	132	142	73
From other countries	43	109	167	222	125	145	174	123	127	162	250	240
Total exports	858	628	709	546	350	288	316	492	393	267	276	137
To CMEA	462	173	163	165	143	96	113	222	135	175	180	75
To other countries	396	455	546	381	207	192	202	271	258	92	96	61
Domestic use of energy	1,938	2,431	2,523	2,745	2,363	2,416	2,393	2,450	2,487	2,576	2,687	2,596
Of which:												
Electricity generation	242	275	296	391	251	116	150	84	98	83	90	123
Other purposes	1,696	2,157	2,227	2,355	2,113	2,301	2,243	2,366	2,389	2,493	2,597	2,472
Of which:												
Industry	1,067	1,683	18	1,877	1,584	1,501	1,443	1,447	1,469	1,536	1,599	1,555
Agriculture	141	165	175	182	166	157	156	168	181	184	191	193
Households	220	230	246	253	242	244	260	268	270	258	265	275
Others	268	70	58	42	120	399	384	484	469	515	542	449

Source: Ministry of Heavy Industry, Mining and Energy.

Table A6. Domestic Production of Energy, 1975–90
(In thousand tons of oil equivalent)

Item	1975	1980	1981	1982	1983	1984	1985	1986	1987	1988	1989	1990
Coal	296	397	405	443	480	536	562	576	579	600	579	574
Bituminous coal	19	32	34	41	40	47	48	44	51	38	46	45
Wood	270	268	272	279	264	254	276	273	276	264	266	281
Oil	1,829	1,388	1,352	1,246	1,173	1,280	1,188	1,205	1,182	1,167	1,129	1,067
Gas	243	592	683	798	333	116	173	223	201	158	198	206
Electricity	142	324	381	341	255	299	272	439	378	342	356	274
Of which:												
Hydropower stations	84	258	299	248	195	271	235	419	354	323	334	245
Total domestic sources	2,741	2,935	3,045	3,054	2,485	2,505	2,482	2,740	2,644	2,549	2,570	2,418

Source: Ministry of Heavy Industry, Mining and Energy.

Table A7. Production and Consumption of Electric Power, 1975–90
(In million kilowatt-hours)

	1975	1980	1981	1982	1983	1984	1985	1986	1987	1988	1989	1990
Production of electric power	1,648	3,767	4,434	3,965	2,962	3,477	3,157	5,107	4,393	3,982	4,135	3,190
Of which:												
Thermal	672	763	957	1,085	696	321	416	233	273	231	250	342
Hydro	976	3,004	3,477	2,880	2,266	3,156	2,731	4,874	4,120	3,751	3,885	2,848
Imports	—	—	—	—	—	—	—	5	167	183	147	323
Exports	366	1,223	1,783	1,256	430	758	652	2,093	1,423	736	629	118
Losses in network and station consumption	251	383	451	418	369	394	397	518	508	544	543	567
Domestic consumption	1,031	2,161	2,200	2,291	2,163	2,325	2,108	2,501	2,629	2,885	3,002	2,828
Of which:												
Industry	740	1,679	1,675	1,735	1,648	1,727	1,552	1,815	1,854	2,034	2,149	1,944
Agriculture	68	160	188	213	171	226	222	262	304	333	325	333
Households	110	136	151	161	165	187	193	215	233	250	271	280
Others	113	196	176	182	169	185	141	209	230	268	257	271

Source: Ministry of Heavy Industry, Mining and Energy.

Table A8. Gross Fixed Investment, 1980–90[1]
(In millions of leks at constant 1986 prices)

	1980	1981	1982	1983	1984	1985	1986	1987	1988	1989	1990
Material sphere	3,011	3,363	3,581	3,775	3,805	3,432	3,555	3,647	3,702	4,183	3,430
Agriculture	1,004	1,280	1,384	1,417	1,357	1,253	1,357	1,330	1,356	1,526	1,373
Electricity	142	115	168	265	409	400	161	182	94	106	104
Industry (other than electricity)	1,129	1,290	1,179	1,279	1,289	1,078	1,233	1,326	1,429	1,758	1,231
Mining	308	323	424	415	402	435	451	489	513	420	435
Transport	314	269	281	267	224	166	212	210	214	260	180
Trade	42	35	58	46	41	34	41	48	50	53	58
Other	72	51	87	86	83	66	100	62	46	60	49
Nonmaterial sphere	917	695	815	781	700	675	697	704	730	732	787
Housing	197	192	247	257	215	220	229	235	227	238	237
Other	720	503	568	524	485	455	468	469	503	494	550
Total	3,928	4,058	4,396	4,556	4,505	4,107	4,252	4,351	4,432	4,915	4,217

Source: Department of Statistics, State Planning Commission.
[1] Excluding military and some other unidentified expenditures.

Table A9. Employment by Sector, 1975–90
(In thousands, annual averages)

	1975	1980	1981	1982	1983	1984	1985	1986	1987	1988	1989	1990
Total employment	893	1,122	1,161	1,216	1,252	1,279	1,298	1,341	1,381	1,405	1,431	1,434
State sector	503	655	676	709	735	757	769	800	830	852	881	906
Cooperatives sector	390	467	485	507	517	522	529	541	551	553	550	528
Material sphere	772	944	976	1,022	1,051	1,071	1,085	1,127	1,158	1,173	1,192	1,189
Agriculture, forestry	457	559	577	597	615	631	645	672	696	706	707	704
Industry	180	238	249	263	271	277	281	292	307	312	325	325
Transport and communications	19	22	24	26	27	28	29	31	31	30	29	29
Trade and catering	17	19	20	20	21	21	21	22	21	22	25	25
Construction	92	99	99	108	109	106	101	102	95	95	99	99
Other	7	7	7	8	8	8	8	8	8	7	7	7
Nonmaterial sphere	121	178	185	194	201	208	213	214	223	232	239	245
Education	43	50	51	52	54	56	56	57	59	61	63	65
Health	24	33	33	34	35	35	36	38	38	39	41	43
Public services (transport, trade)	37	41	45	48	52	54	56	54	58	64	65	67
Scientific research institutions	. . .	. . .	. . .	. . .	. . .	. . .	. . .	2	3	3	3	3
Central Government	. . .	. . .	. . .	. . .	. . .	. . .	. . .	9	10	12	11	11
Specialized organizations[1]	. . .	. . .	. . .	. . .	. . .	. . .	. . .	4	4	4	4	4
Other	17	54	56	60	60	63	65	50	51	49	52	52
Memorandum item:												
Average number of hours worked per week	48	48	48	48	48	48	48	48	48	48	48	48

Source: Statistical Directorate and Employment Directorate, State Planning Commission.
[1]Social and political organizations.

Table A10. Selected Retail Prices in Official and Private Markets
(In leks per kilogram)[1]

	1990				1991					
	March	June	September	December	January	February	March	April	May	June
Dried onions										
Official market	2.4	. . .	2.2	3.0	3.0	3.0	3.0	3.0	4.0	. . .
Private market	3.5	. . .	3.0	4.0	5.0	6.0	6.0	5.0	6.0	. . .
Difference (in percent)	45.8	. . .	36.4	33.3	66.7	100.0	100.0	66.7	50.0	. . .
Dried garlic										
Official market	10.0	. . .	10.0	10.0	10.0	10.0	. . .	. . .	. . .	. . .
Private market	14.0	. . .	14.0	14.0	15.0	15.0	. . .	. . .	. . .	. . .
Difference (in percent)	40.0	. . .	40.0	40.0	50.0	50.0	. . .	. . .	. . .	. . .
Fresh onions										
Official market	2.0	1.6	. . .	. . .	2.5	2.5	2.5	2.5	2.0	2.5
Private market	3.0	2.0	. . .	. . .	3.5	3.5	3.5	3.5	3.0	3.5
Difference (in percent)	50.0	25.0	. . .	. . .	40.0	40.0	40.0	40.0	50.0	40.0
Potatoes										
Official market	3.0	3.0	3.0	3.0	3.0	3.0	3.0	3.0	3.0	3.0
Private market	4.0	4.0	4.0	4.0	5.0	6.0	6.0	6.0	4.0	4.0
Difference (in percent)	33.3	33.3	33.3	33.3	66.7	100.0	100.0	100.0	33.3	33.3
Spinach										
Official market	1.4	. . .	. . .	. . .	1.3	1.8	2.0	2.0	1.5	1.5
Private market	2.5	. . .	. . .	. . .	2.5	2.5	3.0	3.0	1.8	1.8
Difference (in percent)	78.6	. . .	. . .	. . .	92.3	38.9	50.0	50.0	20.0	20.0
Eggs										
Official market	0.9	1.0	1.0	1.0	1.0	1.0	1.0	1.0	1.0	1.0
Private market	1.0	1.0	1.0	1.3	1.3	1.5	1.2	1.2	1.3	1.3
Difference (in percent)	11.1	—	—	30.0	30.0	50.0	20.0	20.0	30.0	30.0
Leeks										
Official market	2.0	. . .	. . .	1.8	2.5	2.6	. . .	. . .	. . .	. . .
Private market	3.0	. . .	. . .	2.0	3.0	4.0	. . .	. . .	. . .	. . .
Difference (in percent)	50.0	. . .	. . .	11.1	20.0	53.8	. . .	. . .	. . .	. . .
Meat										
Official market	17.0	17.0	17.0	17.0	17.0	17.0	17.0	17.0	17.0	17.0
Private market	30.0	30.0	30.0	30.0	33.0	34.0	33.0	33.0	33.0	33.0
Difference (in percent)	76.5	76.5	76.5	76.5	94.1	100.0	94.1	94.1	94.1	94.1

Source: Ministry of Internal Trade.
[1] Except for the price of eggs, which refers to leks per piece.

Table A11. State Budget Operations, 1982–90
(In millions of leks)

	1982	1983	1984	1985	1986	1987	1988	1989	1990
I. Total revenue	8,604.0	8,363.0	8,403.0	8,533.0	8,473.0	8,488.0	9,052.0	9,003.0	7,630.0
Tax revenue	7,400.0	7,252.0	7,463.0	7,694.0	7,828.0	7,978.0	7,707.0	8,250.0	7,090.0
Turnover tax	3,586.0	3,462.0	3,210.0	3,321.0	3,883.0	3,934.0	3,880.0	4,224.0	3,936.0
Income tax	3,239.0	3,145.0	2,561.0	2,600.0	1,999.0	1,972.0	1,837.0	2,067.0	1,335.0
Profit transfer from state enterprises	3,128.0	3,020.0	2,443.0	2,467.0	1,870.0	1,864.0	1,749.0	1,974.0	1,273.0
Tax on income of agricultural cooperatives	111.0	125.0	118.0	133.0	129.0	108.0	88.0	93.0	62.0
Social security contribution	575.0	645.0	661.0	668.0	822.0	863.0	889.0	922.0	967.0
Transfer of amortization	—	—	1,031.0	1,105.0	1,124.0	1,209.0	1,101.0	1,037.0	852.0
Nontax revenue	1,204.0	1,111.0	1,391.0	839.0	645.0	510.0	1,345.0	753.0	540.0
Income from budgetary institutions	293.0	293.0	206.0	202.0	200.0	203.0	161.0	156.0	162.0
Tax on foreign trade	322.0	—	—	—	—	—	—	—	—
Confiscation of enterprise deposits	—	—	—	—	—	—	150.0	48.0	—
Use of Emergency Fund	—	—	—	—	—	—	650.0	120.0	—
Other	589.0	818.0	734.0	637.0	445.0	307.0	384.0	429.0	378.0
II. Current expenditure	3,946.5	4,227.9	4,183.9	4,417.8	4,123.0	4,397.0	4,753.7	5,162.6	6,272.4
Wage bill	1,059.5	1,092.7	1,123.8	1,128.7	1,176.0	1,209.0	1,216.7	1,238.0	1,293.4
Wages	969.5	1,002.7	1,029.8	1,034.7	1,064.0	1,091.0	1,099.7	1,120.0	1,169.4
Social security contribution	90.0	90.0	94.0	94.0	112.0	118.0	117.0	118.0	124.0
Interest payment (external)	34.0	32.0	31.0	30.0	25.0	26.0	25.0	70.0	24.0
Operation and maintenance	764.0	784.0	794.0	795.0	653.0	703.0	694.0	738.0	803.0
Material sphere	295.0	309.0	307.0	307.0	167.0	182.0	183.0	239.0	261.0
Nonmaterial sphere	469.0	475.0	487.0	488.0	486.0	521.0	511.0	499.0	542.0
Total subsidies	1,127.0	1,252.2	1,072.1	1,225.1	998.0	1,164.0	1,449.0	1,616.6	2,619.0
Subsidies to enterprises	719.0	968.2	788.1	907.1	738.0	841.0	1,149.0	1,241.6	2,321.0
Budgeted	719.0	629.0	543.0	592.0	635.0	486.0	396.0	506.0	253.0
Extrabudgetary	—	339.2	245.1	315.1	103.0	355.0	753.0	735.6	2,068.0
Price subsidies	363.0	284.0	264.0	280.0	229.0	323.0	286.0	314.0	290.0
Transfers to State Agricultural Bank	45.0	—	20.0	38.0	31.0	—	14.0	61.0	8.0
Social security	778.0	884.0	971.0	1,035.0	1,106.0	1,162.0	1,236.0	1,331.0	1,426.0
Other	184.0	183.0	192.0	204.0	165.0	133.0	133.0	169.0	107.0
III. Total investment	4,630.5	4,670.2	4,901.2	4,412.3	4,440.0	4,440.0	4,491.3	5,474.0	4,197.6
Budgeted	4,630.5	4,457.3	4,901.2	4,412.3	4,440.0	4,440.0	4,314.3	4,467.0	3,684.6
Extrabudgetary	—	212.9	—	—	—	—	177.0	1,007.0	513.0
IV. Funds of Council of Ministers and branch ministries (+: net use of funds)	9.6	114.9	61.8	58.1	−81.3	−60.9	10.9	−32.9	−138.5
V. Total expenditures (II+III+IV)	8,586.6	9,013.0	9,146.9	8,888.2	8,481.7	8,776.1	9,255.9	10,603.7	10,331.5
VI. Fiscal balance, commitment basis	17.4	−650.0	−743.9	−355.2	−8.7	−288.1	−203.9	−1,600.7	−2,701.5
(as percent of GDP)	0.1	−3.9	−4.5	−2.1	−0.1	−1.7	−1.2	−8.6	−16.6
VII. Government arrears to enterprises	—	—	366.1	−366.1	—	—	175.5	571.7	1,928.2
VIII. Fiscal balance, cash basis	17.4	−650.0	−377.8	−721.3	−8.7	−288.1	−28.4	−1,029.0	−773.3
(as percent of GDP)	0.1	−3.9	−2.3	−4.3	−0.1	−1.7	−0.2	−5.5	−4.8
IX. Financing requirement (+)	−17.4	650.0	377.8	721.3	8.7	288.1	28.4	1,029.0	773.3
X. Domestic financing (+: increase)									
Net position versus Bank	−119.2	668.3	377.8	521.0	36.7	248.4	28.4	1,029.0	773.3
Deposits[1]	53.9	−471.3	−356.7	−818.8	93.5	79.2	−75.1	−880.6	171.2
Reserve Account	51.7	−368.7	−305.4	−770.7	7.9	12.9	−74.0	−923.5	22.7
Gold and precious metal fund[2]	11.8	12.3	10.5	10.0	4.3	5.4	9.8	10.0	10.0
Council of Ministers; branch ministries	−9.6	−114.9	−61.8	−58.1	81.3	60.9	−10.9	32.9	138.5
Credit[3]	−65.3	197.0	21.1	−297.8	130.2	327.6	−46.7	148.4	944.5
Advances to government	—	186.2	−87.1	−89.4	93.2	252.4	−126.9	249.1	771.6
Overdraft facility	−65.3	10.8	108.2	−208.4	37.0	75.2	80.2	−100.7	172.9
XI. External financing	—	—	—	—	—	—	—	—	—
Foreign loans									
Amortization (−)	—	—	—	—	—	—	—	—	—
XII. Errors and omissions (VI−VII−VIII) (+: overfinancing)	101.8	−18.3	−0.0	200.3	−28.0	−39.7	—	—	—
Memorandum item:									
Accumulated government arrears to enterprises	—	—	366.1	—	—	—	175.5	747.2	2,675.4

Source: Ministry of Finance.
[1]A negative sign indicates a reduction in deposits.
[2]Valued at constant 1982 prices.
[3]A negative sign indicates a reduction in credit.

Table A12. General Government Tax Revenue
(In percent of total tax revenue)

	1982	1983	1984	1985	1986	1987	1988	1989	1990
Total Tax Revenue	100.0	100.0	100.0	100.0	100.0	100.0	100.0	100.0	100.0
Turnover tax	48.5	47.7	43.0	43.2	49.6	49.3	50.3	51.2	55.5
Income tax	43.8	43.4	34.3	33.8	25.5	24.7	23.8	25.1	18.8
Profit transfer from state enterprises	42.3	41.6	32.7	32.1	23.9	23.4	22.7	23.9	18.0
Tax on income of agricultural cooperatives	1.5	1.7	1.6	1.7	1.6	1.4	1.1	1.1	0.9
Social security contributions	7.8	8.9	8.9	8.7	10.5	10.8	11.5	11.2	13.6
Transfer of amortization	—	—	13.8	14.4	14.4	15.2	14.3	12.6	12.0
Total enterprise transfer (Profit and amortization transfer)	42.3	41.6	46.5	46.4	38.2	38.5	37.0	36.5	30.0
(In percent of GDP)									
Total Tax Revenue	44.7	43.4	45.2	45.6	45.0	46.2	45.3	44.2	43.7
Turnover tax	21.7	20.7	19.4	19.7	22.3	22.8	22.8	22.6	24.2
Income tax	19.6	18.8	15.5	15.4	11.5	11.4	10.8	11.1	8.2
Profit transfer from state enterprises	18.9	18.1	14.8	14.6	10.8	10.8	10.3	10.6	7.8
Tax on income of agricultural cooperatives	0.7	0.7	0.7	0.8	0.7	0.6	0.5	0.5	0.4
Social security contributions	3.5	3.9	4.0	4.0	4.7	5.0	5.2	4.9	6.0
Transfer of amortization	—	—	6.2	6.6	6.5	7.0	6.5	5.6	5.2
Total enterprise transfer (Profit and amortization transfer)	18.9	18.1	21.0	21.2	17.2	17.8	16.8	16.1	13.1

Source: Ministry of Finance.

Table A13. General Government Expenditure
(In percent of total expenditure)

	1982	1983	1984	1985	1986	1987	1988	1989	1990
Current expenditure	46.0	46.9	43.6	49.7	48.6	50.1	51.4	48.7	60.7
Wage bill	12.3	12.1	11.7	12.7	13.9	13.8	13.1	11.7	12.5
Wages	11.3	11.1	10.7	11.6	12.5	12.4	11.9	10.6	11.3
Social security contributions	1.0	1.0	1.0	1.1	1.3	1.3	1.3	1.1	1.2
Interest payment (external)	0.4	0.4	0.3	0.3	0.3	0.3	0.3	0.7	0.2
Operation and maintenance	8.9	8.7	8.3	8.9	7.7	8.0	7.5	7.0	7.8
Total subsidies	13.1	13.9	11.2	13.8	11.8	13.3	15.7	15.2	25.3
Subsidies to enterprises	8.4	10.7	8.2	10.2	8.7	9.6	12.4	11.7	22.5
Budgeted	8.4	7.0	5.7	6.7	7.5	5.5	4.3	4.8	2.4
Extrabudgetary	—	3.8	2.6	3.5	1.2	4.0	8.1	6.9	20.0
Price subsidies	4.2	3.2	2.8	3.2	2.7	3.7	3.1	3.0	2.8
Social security	9.1	9.8	10.1	11.6	13.0	13.2	13.4	12.6	13.8
Total investment	53.9	51.8	55.8	49.6	52.3	50.6	48.5	51.6	40.6
Budgeted	53.9	49.5	51.1	49.6	52.3	50.6	46.6	42.1	35.7
Extrabudgetary	—	2.4	4.7	—	—	—	1.9	9.5	5.0
Use of funds of Council of Ministers and branch ministries (−: revenue)	0.1	1.3	0.6	0.7	−1.0	−0.7	0.1	−0.3	−1.3
Total expenditure	100.0	100.0	100.0	100.0	100.0	100.0	100.0	100.0	100.0
					(In percent of GDP)				
Current expenditure	23.9	25.3	25.3	26.2	23.7	25.5	27.9	27.6	38.6
Wage bill	6.4	6.5	6.8	6.7	6.8	7.0	7.2	6.6	8.0
Wages	5.9	6.0	6.2	6.1	6.1	6.3	6.5	6.0	7.2
Social security contributions	0.5	0.5	0.6	0.6	0.6	0.7	0.7	0.6	0.8
Interest payment (external)	0.2	0.2	0.2	0.2	0.1	0.2	0.1	0.4	0.1
Operation and maintenance	4.6	4.7	4.8	4.7	3.8	4.1	4.1	4.0	4.9
Total subsidies	6.8	7.5	6.5	7.3	5.7	6.7	8.5	8.7	16.1
Subsidies to enterprises	4.3	5.8	4.8	5.4	4.2	4.9	6.8	6.6	14.3
Budgeted	4.3	3.8	3.3	3.5	3.7	2.8	2.3	2.7	1.6
Extrabudgetary	—	2.0	1.5	1.9	0.6	2.1	4.4	3.9	12.7
Price subsidies	2.2	1.7	1.6	1.7	1.3	1.9	1.7	1.7	1.8
Social security	4.7	5.3	5.9	6.1	6.4	6.7	7.3	7.1	8.8
Total investment	28.0	27.9	32.4	26.2	25.5	25.7	26.4	29.3	25.9
Budgeted	28.0	26.7	29.7	26.2	25.5	25.7	25.4	23.9	22.7
Extrabudgetary	—	1.3	—	—	—	—	1.0	5.4	3.2
Use of funds of Council of Ministers and branch ministries (−: revenue)	0.1	0.7	0.4	0.3	−0.5	−0.4	0.1	−0.2	−0.9
Total expenditure	51.9	53.9	55.4	52.7	48.8	50.9	54.4	56.8	63.6

Source: Ministry of Finance.

Table A14. State Investment
(In millions of leks)

	1982	1983	1984	1985	1986	1987	1988	1989	1990
Investment for the material sphere	3,706.0	3,781.9	3,919.0	3,441.0	3,429.0	3,418.0	3,483.0	4,440.0	3,041.0
Budgeted	3,706.0	3,569.0	3,919.0	3,441.0	3,429.0	3,418.0	3,306.0	3,433.0	2,528.0
Extrabudgetary	—	212.9	—	—	—	—	177.0	1,007.0	513.0
Investment for the nonmaterial sphere	924.5	888.3	982.2	971.3	1,011.0	1,022.0	1,008.3	1,034.0	1,156.6
Defense	684.0	693.0	761.0	749.0	769.0	805.0	750.0	750.0	722.0
Ministry of Interior	59.5	64.3	71.2	90.3	84.0	86.0	87.3	96.0	185.6
All other	181.0	131.0	150.0	132.0	158.0	131.0	171.0	188.0	249.0
Total investment	4,630.5	4,670.2	4,901.2	4,412.3	4,440.0	4,440.0	4,491.3	5,474.0	4,197.6
(as percent of GDP)	28.0	27.9	29.7	26.2	25.5	25.7	26.4	29.3	25.9

Source: Ministry of Finance.

Table A15. Consumer Price Subsidies
(In millions of leks)

	1982	1983	1984	1985	1986	1987	1988	1989	1990
Childwear	14.0	11.0	11.0	11.0	9.0	13.0	27.0	12.0	14.0
Cereals	130.0	131.0	109.0	103.0	112.0	136.0	98.0	146.0	104.0
Meat	65.0	71.0	88.0	71.0	58.0	120.0	92.0	92.0	113.0
Subsidy for general price reduction	137.0	39.0	12.0	10.0	10.0	—	7.0	—	1.0
Flour	—	16.0	20.0	15.0	12.0	23.0	17.0	12.0	15.0
Fertilizer	—	10.0	9.0	11.0	13.0	19.0	14.0	17.0	21.0
Other	17.0	6.0	15.0	59.0	15.0	12.0	31.0	35.0	22.0
Total price subsidy	363.0	284.0	264.0	280.0	229.0	323.0	286.0	314.0	290.0
(as percent of GDP)	2.2	1.7	1.6	1.7	1.3	1.9	1.7	1.7	1.8

Source: Ministry of Finance.

Table A16. Subsidies to Enterprises
(In millions of leks)

		1982	1983	1984	1985	1986	1987	1988	1989	1990
I.	Budgeted Subsidies	719.0	629.0	543.0	592.0	635.0	486.0	396.0	506.0	253.0
	For increasing working capital	260.0	197.0	193.0	188.0	131.0	187.0	143.0	35.0	—
	For covering profit loss	104.0	63.0	131.0	177.0	150.0	154.0	82.0	197.0	12.0
	To agricultural machine stations[1]	255.0	269.0	119.0	127.0	67.0	17.0	26.0	118.0	121.0
	To retail distributors[2]	100.0	100.0	100.0	100.0	118.0	128.0	145.0	156.0	120.0
	Planned general subsidies	—	—	—	—	169.0	—	—	—	—
II.	Extrabudgetary Subsidies	—	339.2	245.1	315.1	103.0	355.0	753.0	502.8	2,068.0
	Extrabudgetary subsidies for above categories[3]	—	153.0	146.0	315.0	—	—	525.0	500.0	1,717.0
	Foreign trade subsidy[4]	—	186.2	99.1	0.1	103.0	355.0	228.0	2.8	351.0
III.	Net Subsidies Due to Reforms	—	—	—	—	—	—	—	232.8	—
IV.	Total Enterprise Subsidy	719.0	968.2	788.1	907.1	738.0	841.0	1,149.0	1,241.6	2,321.0
	(as percent of GDP)	4.3	5.8	4.8	5.4	4.2	4.9	6.8	6.6	14.3

Source: Ministry of Finance.
[1]Since 1989, net of revenues.
[2]Until 1986, retailers withheld their budget subsidy from the turnover tax collected by them. Estimate by the Ministry of Finance is leks 100 million per year.
[3]The bulk is directed to cover losses.
[4]Transferred to the central bank, to cover differences between the domestic currency value of foreign trade transactions converted at the official exchange rate and the domestic currency value at wholesale prices paid (or received) by the central bank to (from) foreign trade enterprises.

Table A17. Net Transfers of Enterprise Sector to State Budget
(In percent of GDP)

	1982	1983	1984	1985	1986	1987	1988	1989	1990
Total enterprise transfers	18.9	18.1	21.0	21.2	17.2	17.8	17.6	16.4	13.1
Profit tax	18.9	18.1	14.8	14.6	10.8	10.8	10.3	10.6	7.8
Remittance of bank deposits	—	—	—	—	—	—	0.9	0.3	—
Amortization[1]	—	—	6.2	6.6	6.5	7.0	6.5	5.6	5.2
Total enterprise subsidies	4.3	5.8	4.8	5.4	4.2	4.9	6.8	6.6	14.3
Net transfers to budget	14.6	12.3	16.3	15.8	13.0	12.9	10.9	9.7	−1.2

Source: Ministry of Finance.
[1] Until 1983 amortization transfer was lumped together with profit taxes.

Table A18. Balance Sheet of State Bank of Albania (SBA), 1980–90
(In millions of leks; end of period)

	1980	1981	1982	1983	1984	1985	1986	1987	1988	1989	1990
Assets											
Foreign assets	630.5	708.1	666.9	546.0	513.5	529.5	630.8	720.6	1,540.2	3,645.2	1,961.1
Gold	354.1	363.3	370.3	365.1	386.4	472.5	477.2	483.2	285.6	258.6	188.2
Convertible currencies	275.5	343.7	296.4	180.7	126.9	56.7	153.4	237.3	1,254.4	3,386.4	1,772.8
Nonconvertible currencies	1.0	1.2	0.2	0.2	0.1	0.3	0.3	0.1	0.2	0.2	0.2
Claims on State Agricultural Bank	952.0	993.0	949.0	898.0	1,053.0	915.0	1,369.0	1,531.0	1,739.0	1,661.0	2,084.0
Domestic credit	5,959.5	6,260.3	6,529.6	6,466.3	5,988.7	5,958.9	5,711.5	6,011.3	5,794.8	6,083.3	6,753.1
To state enterprises	5,865.0	6,168.0	6,438.9	6,377.2	5,901.4	5,873.1	5,626.1	5,926.4	5,711.2	6,000.0	6,671.2
To individuals	94.5	92.3	90.8	89.1	87.2	85.8	85.5	84.9	83.6	83.4	81.9
Other assets	83.1	85.9	91.4	108.8	98.5	135.2	134.9	142.2	122.6	133.7	136.1
Total assets	7,625.1	8,047.2	8,237.0	8,019.1	7,653.7	7,538.6	7,846.3	8,405.0	9,196.5	11,523.2	10,934.4
Liabilities											
Currency in circulation	703.3	757.3	800.2	911.2	944.5	967.1	1,035.2	1,162.4	1,233.9	1,241.7	1,694.9
Foreign liabilities	157.0	259.2	168.8	111.6	108.3	78.3	143.3	222.8	1,390.0	4,414.9	4,684.8
Convertible currencies	6.8	12.3	6.6	7.8	8.7	10.9	15.8	21.9	917.2	4,020.0	3,889.6
Foreign banks	—	—	—	—	—	—	—	—	889.6	3,981.6	2,136.8
Arrears	—	—	—	—	—	—	—	—	—	—	1,648.0
Local embassies	6.8	12.3	6.6	7.8	8.7	10.9	15.8	21.9	27.6	38.4	104.8
Nonconvertible currencies	150.3	247.0	162.2	103.8	99.6	67.5	127.6	197.1	468.9	391.4	794.0
Domestic currency	—	—	—	—	—	—	—	3.8	3.9	3.5	1.2
Liabilities to government (net)	3,951.4	3,895.0	4,014.3	3,345.9	2,968.0	2,559.7	2,523.1	2,274.8	2,246.4	1,336.3	651.2
Reserve Account balance	3,288.1	3,174.1	3,225.8	2,857.1	2,551.7	1,781.0	1,788.9	1,801.8	1,727.8	804.3	827.0
Gold and precious metals	415.7	427.6	439.4	451.7	462.2	584.9	589.2	594.8	604.4	733.3	831.6
Deposits and other liabilities	294.0	330.7	321.1	206.2	144.4	86.3	167.6	228.5	217.6	250.5	389.0
Claims on government[1]	−46.5	−37.4	27.9	−186.2	−99.1	−9.7	−102.9	−355.3	−228.4	−477.5	−1,249.1
Transaction account balances (net)				17.1	−91.1	117.3	80.3	5.1	−75.1	25.6	−147.3
Liabilities to savings banks	787.6	818.2	881.1	983.8	1,069.4	1,160.4	1,263.5	1,405.5	1,562.4	1,645.1	1,786.2
Deposits	1,000.9	894.3	752.0	817.8	785.5	704.9	834.2	777.5	880.4	1,280.7	1,599.4
State enterprises	1,000.9	894.3	752.0	817.8	785.5	704.9	834.2	777.5	879.7	1,278.5	1,595.1
Domestic	1,000.9	894.3	752.0	817.8	785.5	704.9	834.2	777.5	879.7	1,278.5	1,588.9
Foreign currency	—	—	—	—	—	—	—	—	—	—	6.2
Individuals	—	—	—	—	—	—	—	—	0.7	2.2	4.3
Foreign currency	—	—	—	—	—	—	—	—	0.7	2.2	4.3
Other liabilities	1,024.9	1,423.3	1,620.7	1,848.8	1,778.1	2,068.1	2,047.0	2,562.0	1,883.6	1,604.5	517.9
Capital	750.0	750.0	750.0	750.0	750.0	750.0	750.0	750.0	750.0	750.0	750.0
Reserves	250.0	250.0	250.0	250.0	250.0	250.0	250.0	250.0	250.0	250.0	250.0
Strategic commodity reserve	—	—	—	—	—	—	—	650.0	120.0	—	—
Other identified items	541.6	799.5	779.6	696.8	464.2	549.1	560.3	497.6	415.1	824.8	−993.6
Unidentified residual	−516.7	−376.2	−158.9	152.0	313.9	519.0	486.7	414.4	348.4	−220.3	511.5
Total liabilities	7,625.1	8,047.2	8,237.0	8,019.1	7,653.7	7,538.6	7,846.3	8,405.0	9,196.5	11,523.2	10,934.4
Memorandum item:											
Liabilities to government (net), excluding revaluations	3,951.4	3,895.0	4,014.3	3,345.9	2,968.0	2,447.0	2,410.3	2,162.1	2,133.6	1,104.6	331.2

Source: State Bank of Albania.
[1] Comprises transfers of funds to the state enterprises by the SBA on behalf of the government, SBA losses due to foreign trade transactions, and SBA loans denominated in foreign exchange to the Ministry of Trade to finance imports of capital equipment.

Table A19. Balance Sheet of State Agricultural Bank, 1980–90
(In millions of leks; end of period)

	1980	1981	1982	1983	1984	1985	1986	1987	1988	1989	1990
Assets											
Domestic credit	1,828.0	1,976.0	2,036.0	2,010.0	2,119.0	2,106.0	2,508.0	2,692.0	2,833.0	3,007.0	3,351.0
To state farms	689.0	677.0	710.0	712.0	765.0	800.0	993.0	1,085.0	1,175.0	1,317.0	1,538.0
To cooperatives	1,127.0	1,284.0	1,306.0	1,271.0	1,318.0	1,260.0	1,458.0	1,536.0	1,573.0	1,590.0	1,700.0
To individuals	12.0	15.0	20.0	27.0	36.0	46.0	57.0	71.0	85.0	100.0	113.0
Other assets	6.0	4.0	1.0	2.0	1.0	1.0	1.0	1.0	1.0	1.0	16.0
Total assets	1,834.0	1,980.0	2,037.0	2,012.0	2,120.0	2,107.0	2,509.0	2,693.0	2,834.0	3,008.0	3,367.0
Liabilities											
Deposits	266.0	317.0	348.0	360.0	330.0	430.0	351.0	378.0	339.0	425.0	463.0
State farms	62.0	69.0	73.0	96.0	75.0	69.0	65.0	78.0	83.0	76.0	104.0
Cooperatives	204.0	248.0	275.0	264.0	255.0	361.0	286.0	300.0	256.0	349.0	359.0
Government funding	327.0	355.0	400.0	412.0	432.0	432.0	463.0	480.0	494.0	555.0	562.0
Liabilities to State Bank	952.0	993.0	949.0	898.0	1,053.0	915.0	1,369.0	1,531.0	1,739.0	1,661.0	2,084.0
Other liabilities	289.0	315.0	340.0	342.0	305.0	330.0	326.0	304.0	262.0	367.0	258.0
Capital	250.0	250.0	250.0	250.0	250.0	250.0	250.0	250.0	250.0	250.0	250.0
Other	39.0	65.0	90.0	92.0	55.0	80.0	76.0	54.0	12.0	117.0	8.0
Total liabilities	1,834.0	1,980.0	2,037.0	2,012.0	2,120.0	2,107.0	2,509.0	2,693.0	2,834.0	3,008.0	3,367.0

Source: State Bank of Albania.

Table A20. Balance Sheet of Savings Banks, 1980–90
(In millions of leks; end of period)

	1980	1981	1982	1983	1984	1985	1986	1987	1988	1989	1990
Assets											
Deposits with SBA	787.6	818.2	881.1	983.8	1,069.4	1,160.4	1,263.5	1,405.5	1,562.4	1,645.1	1,786.2
Total assets	787.6	818.2	881.1	983.8	1,069.4	1,160.4	1,263.5	1,405.5	1,562.4	1,645.1	1,786.2
Liabilities											
Deposits of individuals	700.0	735.0	788.0	891.0	985.0	1,071.0	1,183.0	1,329.0	1,478.0	1,567.0	1,707.0
Demand deposits	405.0	415.0	445.0	507.0	558.0	606.0	670.0	755.0	832.0	864.0	917.0
Time deposits	295.0	320.0	343.0	384.0	427.0	465.0	513.0	574.0	646.0	703.0	790.0
Other liabilities[1]	87.6	83.2	93.1	92.8	84.4	89.4	80.5	76.5	84.4	78.1	79.2
Total liabilities	787.6	818.2	881.1	983.8	1,069.4	1,160.4	1,263.5	1,405.5	1,562.4	1,645.1	1,786.2

Source: State Bank of Albania.
[1] Insurance premiums.

Table A21. Interest Rates on Bank Credits,[1] 1980–90
(In percent per annum)

	1980	1981	1982	1983	1984	1985	1986	1987	1988	1989	1990
Working capital credit required for achievement of plan targets[1]	2.0	2.0	2.0	2.0	2.0	2.0	2.0	2.0	2.0	2.0	2.0
Temporary credit[1]	2.0	2.0	2.0	2.0	2.0	2.0	2.0	2.0	2.0	2.0	2.0
Short-term credit for advanced settlement of accounts between enterprises[1]	1.0	1.0	1.0	1.0	1.0	1.0	1.0	1.0	1.0	1.0	1.0
Short-term occasional credit for settlement of accounts between enterprises[2]							2.0			2.0	2.0
Short-term occasional credit to state enterprises for gathering of agricultural production from cooperatives									2.0		
Short-term occasional credit (2–3 months' maturity)									2.0		
Long-term occasional credit (2–3 years' maturity) for financing of unsold and unused inventory stocks			2.0					2.0			
Short-term occasional credit for settlement of interenterprises' arrears											4.0
Credit arrears for financing of unsold and unused inventory stocks[3]									6.0	6.0	

Source: State Bank of Albania.
[1]For state enterprises, state farms, but not agricultural cooperatives.
[2]For state enterprises, state farms, and agricultural cooperatives.
[3]Except for this type of credit, interest rates on other credit arrears are double the respective normal rate.

Table A22. Interest Rates on Bank Deposits,[1] 1980–90
(In percent per annum)

	1980–85	1986–90
Deposits with State Bank of Albania		
Deposits of state enterprises[1]	0.5	0.5
Deposits of savings banks	3.0	3.0
Deposits in foreign currency (U.S. dollar)		
Demand deposits	2.0	6.0
Time deposits (6 months)	2.0	7.0
Time deposits (12 months)	4.0	8.0
Deposits with Agricultural Bank[2]		
Deposits of state farms[1]	0.5	0.5
Deposits of cooperatives[1]	0.5	0.5
Deposits with Savings Banks		
Demand deposits of households	2.0	2.0
Time deposits of households (6 months)	3.0	3.0

Source: State Bank of Albania.
[1]From July 1, 1990 the interest rate on deposits has been increased to 1 percent.
[2]For a selected number of cooperatives receiving credit at zero interest rate, the interest rate on deposits was equal to zero percent until 1990, and
1 percent thereafter.

Table A23. Balance of Payments in Rubles, 1968–90
(In millions of rubles)

	1968	1969	1970	1971	1972	1973	1974	1975	1976	1977	1978	1979	1980	1981	1982	1983	1984	1985	1986	1987	1988	1989	1990
Current account	-33.7	-52.0	-44.7	-25.6	-55.8	-51.5	-1.0	-103.9	-20.3	-60.7	-44.6	17.7	0.1	24.0	-8.4	-1.6	3.1	-5.1	-4.5	-0.6	-13.5	18.8	-44.9
Trade balance	-32.9	-51.6	-44.3	-24.5	-55.2	-51.6	-1.5	-104.8	-20.4	-59.0	-43.5	17.5	0.2	22.0	-10.4	-2.9	-0.6	-9.5	-9.0	-6.3	-18.6	15.0	-48.6
Exports, f.o.b.	54.8	57.9	61.5	75.8	83.0	83.9	103.2	99.0	98.5	72.0	52.9	88.1	98.9	128.5	117.1	136.6	124.4	125.0	157.0	157.4	173.1	206.5	132.4
Imports, f.o.b.	87.7	109.5	105.8	100.3	138.2	135.5	104.7	203.8	118.9	131.0	96.4	70.6	98.7	106.5	127.5	139.5	125.0	134.5	166.0	163.7	191.7	191.5	181.0
Services balance	-0.8	-0.4	-0.4	-1.1	-0.6	0.2	0.5	0.9	0.1	-1.6	-1.0	0.1	-0.1	2.0	2.1	1.4	3.7	4.5	4.5	5.7	5.1	3.8	3.8
Receipts	1.8	2.3	2.4	2.9	3.4	4.3	4.5	4.7	4.7	3.4	3.4	3.9	4.6	5.1	6.2	6.2	7.7	8.3	9.3	10.3	9.8	10.1	9.7
Shipment and other transportation	1.0	1.2	1.5	2.0	2.2	2.8	2.9	2.7	2.9	1.9	2.6	3.2	3.2	4.0	4.2	4.1	5.3	6.1	6.2	6.8	6.4	6.4	5.9
Other	0.8	1.1	0.9	0.9	1.2	1.4	1.6	2.0	1.7	1.5	0.9	0.7	1.4	1.1	2.0	2.1	2.4	2.2	3.1	3.5	3.4	3.6	3.8
Expenditures	2.6	2.7	2.8	4.1	4.0	4.1	4.0	3.7	4.6	5.0	4.4	3.8	4.7	3.0	4.1	4.8	4.0	3.8	4.7	4.7	4.7	6.2	6.0
Shipment and other transportation	0.6	0.6	0.6	1.2	0.8	0.7	0.7	0.2	0.3	0.6	0.5	0.2	0.8	1.1	1.5	2.1	1.2	0.9	1.6	1.4	1.2	2.3	1.6
Insurance	0.4	0.5	0.5	0.5	0.7	0.7	0.5	1.0	0.6	0.7	0.5	0.4	0.5	0.5	0.6	0.7	0.6	0.7	0.8	0.8	1.0	1.0	0.9
Interest	1.3	1.3	1.3	1.9	1.9	2.2	2.2	1.9	3.0	3.1	2.9	2.6	2.6	1.1	1.0	0.8	0.8	0.7	0.7	0.7	0.7	0.5	0.2
Other	0.3	0.3	0.4	0.5	0.5	0.6	0.6	0.6	0.6	0.6	0.6	0.7	0.8	0.4	0.9	1.2	1.4	1.4	1.6	1.7	1.8	2.5	3.2
Unrequited transfers, net	—	—	—	—	—	—	—	—	—	—	—	—	—	—	—	—	—	—	—	—	—	—	—
Capital account	31.2	44.5	37.9	59.8	59.9	60.3	42.1	117.0	80.1	14.1	143.8	-21.5	-6.5	-24.9	11.8	3.1	3.6	7.9	7.0	2.4	17.3	-19.0	46.1
Medium- and long-term, net	30.3	37.1	36.8	59.0	55.5	54.4	61.5	120.1	40.7	63.1	98.3	-6.4	-6.4	-2.6	-2.6	-2.1	-2.1	-2.0	-2.0	-2.0	-2.0	-2.0	-2.0
Credits received	30.3	37.1	36.8	59.0	55.5	54.4	61.5	120.1	40.7	63.1	98.3	-6.4	-6.4	-2.6	-2.6	-2.1	-2.1	-2.0	-2.0	-2.0	-2.0	-2.0	-2.0
Disbursements	34.3	41.0	41.0	64.2	74.6	73.5	76.1	130.6	48.7	91.4	104.7	—	—	—	—	—	—	—	—	—	—	—	—
Repayments	4.0	4.0	4.2	5.2	19.1	19.1	14.7	10.6	8.0	28.3	6.4	6.4	6.4	2.6	2.6	2.1	2.1	2.0	2.0	2.0	2.0	2.0	2.0
Credits extended	—	—	—	—	—	—	—	—	—	—	—	—	—	—	—	—	—	—	—	—	—	—	—
Short-term capital, net	0.8	7.5	1.1	0.7	4.4	5.9	-19.4	-3.1	39.4	-48.9	45.6	-15.1	-0.1	-22.3	14.4	5.2	5.7	9.9	9.1	4.4	19.3	-17.1	48.1
Errors and omissions	2.6	7.5	6.8	-34.1	-4.1	-8.9	-41.1	-13.1	-59.8	46.5	-99.3	3.9	6.4	0.9	-3.4	-1.5	-6.7	-2.8	-2.5	-1.7	-3.8	0.2	-1.3
Overall balance	—	—	—	—	—	—	—	—	—	—	—	—	—	—	—	—	—	—	—	—	—	—	—
Financing of overall balance	—	—	—	—	—	—	—	—	—	—	—	—	—	—	—	—	—	—	—	—	—	—	—
Change in reserves (- increase)	—	—	—	—	—	—	—	—	—	—	—	—	—	—	—	—	—	—	—	—	—	—	—

Source: Data provided by the Albanian authorities and IMF staff estimates.

Table A24. Balance of Payments in Nonconvertible Currencies Other than Ruble, 1968–90
(In millions of U.S. dollars)

	1968	1969	1970	1971	1972	1973	1974	1975	1976	1977	1978	1979	1980	1981	1982	1983	1984	1985	1986	1987	1988	1989	1990
Current account	1.4	-0.6	0.1	-0.1	1.9	3.2	-1.1	10.0	2.8	-2.7	-6.1	-20.3	16.0	25.3	-1.4	3.2	-1.3	-2.2	0.8	-1.9	-16.1	-2.5	-14.4
Trade balance	1.4	-0.5	0.3	0.2	2.3	3.7	-0.9	10.2	3.4	-0.9	-4.9	-17.8	19.0	28.3	1.2	5.0	0.3	0.7	4.3	0.9	-10.3	-1.2	-11.6
Exports, f.o.b.	3.0	3.0	4.4	5.1	9.0	13.7	23.5	27.9	19.4	25.0	25.3	31.3	118.2	96.8	68.0	45.2	45.9	46.2	58.8	53.5	38.9	39.5	30.7
Imports, f.o.b.	1.6	3.5	4.1	4.8	6.7	10.0	24.4	17.7	16.0	25.9	30.2	49.1	99.2	68.5	66.8	40.2	45.6	45.5	54.5	52.6	49.2	40.7	42.3
Services balance	-0.1	—	-0.2	-0.4	-0.4	-0.4	-0.2	-0.2	-0.6	-1.8	-1.2	-2.5	-3.0	-3.0	-2.6	-1.8	-1.6	-2.9	-3.5	-2.9	-5.8	-1.3	-2.8
Receipts	—	—	—	—	—	—	—	—	—	—	—	—	0.9	1.6	1.0	1.2	1.0	0.7	0.9	0.7	1.6	2.2	0.6
Shipment and other transportation	—	—	—	—	—	0.4	0.8	0.2	0.2	0.2	0.1	0.1	0.2	0.4	0.3	0.2	0.1	—	—	—	—	1.4	—
Other	0.3	0.4	0.3	0.3	0.4	0.6	0.7	0.8	0.7	0.6	0.4	0.4	0.6	1.2	0.7	0.9	0.9	0.7	0.9	0.7	1.6	0.8	0.6
Expenditures	0.3	0.4	0.5	0.7	0.8	1.4	1.7	1.3	1.5	2.7	1.7	3.0	3.8	4.6	3.6	3.0	2.6	3.6	4.5	3.6	7.4	3.6	3.5
Shipment and other transportation	—	—	—	—	—	0.4	0.6	0.1	0.4	1.5	0.5	1.4	1.9	1.8	1.5	1.2	1.2	1.6	1.9	0.9	4.0	0.9	0.8
Insurance	—	—	—	—	—	0.1	0.1	0.1	0.1	0.1	0.2	0.2	0.5	0.3	0.3	0.2	0.2	0.2	0.3	0.3	0.2	0.2	0.2
Other	0.3	0.4	0.5	0.7	0.8	1.0	1.0	1.1	1.0	1.0	1.1	1.4	1.5	2.4	1.8	1.6	1.1	1.7	2.2	2.4	3.2	2.5	2.5
Unrequited transfers, net	—	—	—	—	—	—	—	—	—	—	—	—	—	—	—	—	—	—	—	—	—	—	—
Capital account	—	3.0	-0.1	-2.9	-1.3	-1.0	-0.8	-15.1	19.5	-9.9	13.9	10.4	-9.7	-29.9	12.4	-25.8	—	-0.1	-1.9	-0.8	10.7	-6.0	0.6
Medium- and long-term, net	—	—	—	—	—	—	—	—	—	—	—	—	—	—	—	—	—	—	—	—	—	—	—
Credits received	—	—	—	—	—	—	—	—	—	—	—	—	—	—	—	—	—	—	—	—	—	—	—
Credits extended	—	—	—	—	—	—	—	—	—	—	—	—	—	—	—	—	—	—	—	—	—	—	—
Short-term capital, net	—	3.0	-0.1	-2.9	-1.3	-1.0	-0.8	-15.1	19.5	-9.9	13.9	10.4	-9.7	-29.9	12.4	-25.8	—	-0.1	-1.9	-0.8	10.7	-6.0	20.6
Errors and omissions	-1.3	-2.5	—	3.0	-0.6	-2.2	1.9	5.1	-22.3	12.7	-7.8	9.9	-6.3	4.5	-11.1	22.6	1.4	2.3	1.1	2.8	5.4	8.6	-6.2
Overall balance	—	—	—	—	—	—	—	—	—	—	—	—	—	—	—	—	—	—	—	—	—	—	—
Financing of overall balance	—	—	—	—	—	—	—	—	—	—	—	—	—	—	—	—	—	—	—	—	—	—	—
Change in reserves (— increase)	—	—	—	—	—	—	—	—	—	—	—	—	—	—	—	—	—	—	—	—	—	—	—

Source: Data provided by the Albanian authorities and IMF staff estimates.

Table A25. Export and Import Indices for Value, Volume, and Prices

	1970	1980	1985	1986	1987	1988	1989	1990
Exports								
Value								
Total	100	531	480	553	514	476	553	388
Nonconvertible currencies	100	429	408	456	421	383	440	290
Convertible currencies	100	2,972	2,417	2,240	2,122	2,471	2,963	2,492
Volume								
Total	100	486	359	490	401	329	287	250
Nonconvertible currencies	100	543	270	355	317	287	242	144
Convertible currencies	100	372	707	842	581	632	698	940
Unit values								
Total	100	109	134	113	128	145	192	155
Nonconvertible currencies	100	79	151	129	133	133	182	201
Convertible currencies	100	800	342	266	365	391	425	265
Imports								
Value								
Total	100	238	266	221	210	270	308	322
Nonconvertible currencies	100	144	169	168	164	167	175	139
Convertible currencies	100	2,089	2,107	1,163	922	1,840	2,419	3,473
Volume								
Total	100	214	350	335	351	419	436	409
Nonconvertible currencies	100	107	154	216	247	238	245	178
Convertible currencies	100	3,167	4,577	2,915	2,328	3,834	4,094	5,323
Unit values								
Total	100	111	76	66	60	65	71	79
Nonconvertible currencies	100	135	110	78	66	70	71	78
Convertible currencies	100	66	44	40	40	48	59	65

Source: Ministry of Foreign Trade.

Table A26. Commodity Composition of Exports and Imports in Convertible Currencies, SITC Classification[1]
(In millions of U.S. dollars)

SITC Category	Description	1970	1980	1985	1986	1987	1988	1989	1990
						Exports			
0	Food and live animals	0.7	10.9	6.9	11.5	12.8	15.4	16.5	22.5
1	Beverages and tobacco	0.2	1.6	1.8	3.9	7.6	5.5	5.2	8.3
2	Crude materials inedible, except fuels	1.7	16.5	33.6	31.5	21.6	42.2	63.3	43.4
3	Mineral fuels, lubricants, and related materials	1.0	52.2	29.3	23.4	24.0	4.0	0.1	8.3
	Of which:								
33	Petroleum and petroleum products	1.0	52.2	29.3	11.8	14.5	4.0	0.1	8.2
4	Animal and vegetable oils and fats	—	—	—	—	—	—	—	—
5	Chemicals	—	0.4	1.6	1.0	2.5	1.8	2.5	0.7
6	Manufactured goods, classified chiefly by material	1.0	13.3	4.7	7.7	10.2	15.7	17.8	8.9
7	Machinery and transport equipment	—	—	—	—	—	—	—	—
8	Miscellaneous manufactured articles	0.1	4.2	5.9	6.7	7.8	7.7	6.2	5.7
9	Miscellaneous transactions and commodities not classified according to kind	—	—	—	—	—	—	—	—
	Total, SITC 0–9	4.8	99.1	83.9	85.7	86.5	92.3	111.7	97.8
						Imports			
0	Food and live animals	0.6	5.0	5.4	4.3	4.9	17.8	28.6	49.4
1	Beverages and tobacco	—	—	—	—	—	—	—	—
2	Crude materials inedible, except fuels	2.4	21.6	13.4	8.5	9.5	12.4	13.5	16.2
3	Mineral fuels, lubricants, and related materials	—	17.1	19.0	9.4	7.7	11.0	12.2	16.0
	Of which:								
33	Petroleum and petroleum products	—	0.4	0.9	0.5	0.9	—	1.6	1.3
4	Animal and vegetable oils and fats	—	10.0	6.5	4.2	2.4	8.8	11.3	18.5
5	Chemicals	0.3	5.4	5.9	5.5	5.9	7.7	14.0	7.5
6	Manufactured goods, classified chiefly by material	3.4	24.3	15.2	12.1	12.4	17.7	29.6	28.5
7	Machinery and transport equipment[2]	0.2	4.0	25.6	20.4	20.2	17.6	18.9	18.7
8	Miscellaneous manufactured articles	—	1.7	0.2	0.1	—	10.1	0.1	0.1
9	Miscellaneous transactions and commodities not classified according to kind	—	—	—	—	—	—	—	—
	Total, SITC 0–9	6.8	89.5	92.2	65.1	63.9	93.1	129.8	156.1

Source: Ministry of Foreign Trade.
[1]Covers a large majority of exports.
[2]Includes projects.

Table A27. Commodity Composition of Exports and Imports in Nonconvertible Currencies, SITC Classification[1]

(In millions of U.S. dollars)

SITC Category	Description	1970	1980	1985	1986	1987	1988	1989	1990
					Exports				
0	Food and live animals	4.0	18.7	28.8	26.0	25.0	28.4	41.5	29.0
1	Beverages and tobacco	16.0	37.8	48.4	39.8	46.4	41.5	58.1	43.2
2	Crude materials inedible, except fuels	17.0	45.4	35.9	42.9	41.5	45.4	42.6	35.8
3	Mineral fuels, lubricants, and related materials	2.4	84.3	40.0	64.8	51.9	43.8	40.1	11.8
	Of which:								
33	Petroleum and petroleum products	2.4	50.0	12.3	19.6	16.2	16.0	17.5	5.1
4	Animal and vegetable oils and fats	—	—	—	—	—	—	—	—
5	Chemicals	—	0.6	3.2	2.0	2.7	2.0	1.9	1.4
6	Manufactured goods, classified chiefly by material	4.4	18.2	25.4	21.2	22.3	22.7	28.0	26.6
7	Machinery and transport equipment	—	—	—	—	—	—	—	—
8	Miscellaneous manufactured articles	2.2	11.3	10.6	8.9	8.8	9.9	7.9	2.8
9	Miscellaneous transactions and commodities not classified according to kind	—	—	—	—	—	—	—	—
	Total, SITC 0–9	46.1	216.2	192.3	205.7	198.5	193.5	220.0	150.6
					Imports				
0	Food and live animals	8.9	7.4	22.8	17.4	11.2	15.3	12.9	14.4
1	Beverages and tobacco	—	—	—	—	—	—	—	—
2	Crude materials inedible, except fuels	6.9	11.0	11.5	10.0	7.5	8.2	6.4	7.7
3	Mineral fuels, lubricants, and related materials	1.1	3.5	12.2	14.6	17.1	16.7	15.9	8.5
	Of which:								
33	Petroleum and petroleum products	—	0.2	—	—	—	0.9	—	—
4	Animal and vegetable oils and fats	2.8	8.5	8.5	10.3	8.0	8.1	4.9	0.6
5	Chemicals	22.5	4.4	3.9	3.1	2.7	2.6	2.6	1.3
6	Manufactured goods, classified chiefly by material	20.9	62.8	45.2	51.2	40.9	38.5	39.2	34.2
7	Machinery and transport equipment[2]	16.8	21.3	50.6	42.3	56.9	84.1	84.6	66.7
8	Miscellaneous manufactured articles	0.5	2.2	1.1	1.5	1.7	1.1	0.9	0.8
9	Miscellaneous transactions and commodities not classified according to kind	—	—	—	—	—	—	—	—
	Total, SITC 0–9	80.5	121.3	155.8	150.4	146.0	175.6	167.5	134.1

Source: Ministry of Foreign Trade.

[1]Covers a large majority of exports. Exports valued in rubles are converted to dollars using official cross exchange rates.

[2]Includes projects.

Table A28. Geographical Distribution of Exports and Imports, 1975–90
(Current prices, millions of leks)

	1975	1980	1981	1982	1983	1984	1985	1986	1987	1988	1989	1990
Exports, f.o.b.	2,057.8	3,573.4	3,512.8	3,155.7	2,992.1	2,799.9	2,664.8	2,490.1	2,489.6	2,549.2	3,029.1	2,288.5
CMEA countries	1,146.6	1,825.0	1,685.8	1,592.2	1,806.8	1,651.6	1,646.9	1,255.7	1,260.0	1,385.0	1,650.9	1,059.3
Bulgaria	107.6	144.0	142.6	188.2	137.6	142.3	158.6	187.0	187.4	239.3	313.2	189.1
Romania	100.2	471.1	385.7	278.1	387.0	352.5	289.1	235.7	232.0	247.0	274.5	106.9
Czechoslovakia	327.6	414.9	391.4	368.1	432.0	404.4	369.8	301.2	307.7	256.6	345.8	335.6
Hungary	137.0	139.9	189.0	204.2	192.9	207.2	260.5	126.2	154.3	151.7	112.2	128.5
Poland	217.6	340.4	268.4	238.8	240.3	228.2	250.4	175.4	149.6	191.6	202.4	107.2
Former east Germany	178.4	223.7	229.1	183.2	240.1	234.4	223.5	141.0	168.8	209.4	278.4	101.2
Others	78.2	91.1	79.7	131.6	127.0	82.7	95.0	89.2	60.2	89.4	124.4	90.8
Industrial countries	323.3	1,114.6	1,141.7	944.7	761.7	736.5	653.3	714.2	744.4	789.1	984.8	862.5
Former west Germany	29.2	135.4	57.1	71.9	75.3	93.5	79.9	80.4	99.1	108.8	147.6	120.5
Italy	144.2	282.5	294.2	180.8	125.7	105.4	44.4	86.4	109.0	161.4	238.3	205.1
Greece	56.6	338.3	370.4	173.9	102.5	123.8	125.4	169.7	136.3	47.2	89.8	65.8
France	17.1	77.4	104.9	45.5	36.7	41.0	42.1	47.6	49.1	41.9	51.8	32.2
Japan	13.8	16.5	11.2	18.1	14.7	11.3	63.9	30.5	39.1	45.9	52.4	48.8
Austria	20.6	57.9	28.4	55.7	50.7	56.7	41.1	37.4	87.6	137.4	123.6	107.5
Developing countries	587.9	633.8	685.3	618.8	423.6	411.7	364.7	520.2	485.2	375.1	393.4	366.7
Yugoslavia	181.9	499.8	617.7	494.4	335.3	334.3	294.2	347.1	276.9	180.9	149.2	174.0
China	387.9	0.0	0.0	0.0	23.2	19.4	47.8	123.1	151.0	130.7	170.6	111.6
Turkey	8.6	73.0	34.2	24.3	0.9	4.7	7.8	2.2	3.8	4.3	6.9	9.4
Egypt	0.0	11.4	7.4	3.2	10.2	14.3	1.1	26.2	37.6	31.6	34.3	37.9
Others	9.5	49.5	26.1	96.8	54.2	39.0	13.7	21.6	15.9	27.6	32.4	33.8
Imports, c.i.f.	3,728.7	3,616.9	3,390.9	4,026.0	3,527.8	3,257.3	3,175.9	2,665.8	2,649.8	3,217.4	3,792.0	3,796.6
CMEA countries	988.4	1,907.5	1,506.5	1,860.4	1,976.7	1,781.9	1,889.7	1,408.8	1,400.3	1,633.1	1,698.4	1,556.0
Bulgaria	89.4	162.0	139.4	192.6	180.2	137.1	142.7	215.1	210.7	298.3	277.3	253.2
Romania	119.2	391.3	337.2	414.4	397.7	377.8	400.5	226.5	250.3	259.1	265.1	186.0
Czechoslovakia	298.0	472.3	354.2	408.1	428.1	445.3	410.8	328.5	381.8	362.1	329.6	323.8
Hungary	99.4	162.0	183.0	222.7	228.8	197.6	251.5	199.2	150.4	148.6	129.0	132.0
Poland	139.0	324.0	204.2	308.7	371.5	287.4	301.2	201.4	168.0	223.4	230.1	165.9
Former east Germany	144.0	274.3	176.0	196.1	259.3	218.1	235.2	157.5	171.3	236.3	324.1	370.9
Others	99.4	121.5	112.4	118.0	111.1	118.4	148.0	80.6	67.8	105.3	143.2	124.2
Industrial countries	...	1,091.7	1,389.5	1,545.6	1,146.6	1,053.4	899.2	747.1	707.7	1,011.1	1,593.3	1,701.9
Former west Germany	108.1	287.9	311.2	365.0	230.5	178.9	143.8	192.7	178.3	196.4	354.0	297.9
Italy	167.3	204.7	251.3	356.3	240.6	183.1	124.2	124.8	143.5	231.8	330.9	375.8
Greece	38.3	222.5	122.5	135.3	108.6	130.1	202.0	101.0	95.7	157.4	274.5	209.1
France	34.8	41.6	78.3	83.5	136.0	235.7	118.1	46.5	55.0	46.2	65.9	99.5
Japan	13.9	17.8	25.8	90.5	42.7	34.6	6.1	7.7	3.5	3.7	6.6	2.0
Austria	55.7	92.0	138.8	109.8	88.8	93.7	68.6	65.8	68.7	82.3	143.2	225.5
Netherlands	34.8	62.3	70.1	96.4	82.8	66.4	43.5	50.6	64.1	73.7	95.8	86.5
Developing countries	...	617.7	494.9	620.0	404.5	421.9	387.0	509.9	541.8	573.2	500.3	538.7
Yugoslavia	119.0	471.9	380.6	539.0	315.2	341.2	302.4	364.5	258.4	136.5	181.7	186.4
China	2,168.2	...	...	...	15.3	37.8	53.8	105.9	194.0	281.4	166.6	236.5
Turkey	...	80.2	53.1	4.2	2.8	1.8	3.6	4.4	8.8	19.6	38.9	54.1
Egypt	...	8.9	20.9	31.4	7.1	...	...	5.9	47.3	58.2	45.3	44.4
Others	...	56.8	40.2	45.4	64.1	41.2	27.0	29.2	33.3	77.5	67.8	17.3

Source: Ministry of Foreign Trade.

Table A29. Exchange Rates[1]

	1968	1969	1970	1971	1972	1973	1974	1975	1976	1977	1978	1979	1980	1981	1982	1983	1984	1985	1986	1987	1988	1989	1990	1991
Average per period																								
(In leks per U.S. dollar)																								
Official rate	5.00	5.00	5.00	4.99	4.60	4.16	4.10	3.90	4.10	4.10	3.80	3.50	3.30	3.30	3.30	3.30	3.30	3.30	—	—	—	—	—	—
Commercial rate	14.40	14.40	14.40	14.37	13.25	11.98	11.81	11.23	11.81	11.81	10.94	10.08	9.50	8.58	8.58	8.58	8.58	8.58	8.00	8.00	8.00	8.00	8.50[2]	10.00
Noncommercial rate	10.00	10.00	10.00	9.97	9.20	8.32	8.20	7.80	8.20	8.20	7.80	7.00	7.00	7.00	7.00	7.00	7.00	7.00	7.00	7.00	7.00	7.00	15.00[3]	15.00
(In leks per ruble)																								
Official rate	5.5555	5.5555	5.5555	5.5555	5.5555	5.5555	5.5555	5.5555	5.5555	5.5555	5.5555	5.5555	5.00	4.92	4.40	4.40	4.40	4.40	—	—	—	—	—	—
Commercial rate	16	16	16	16	16	16	16	16	16	16	16	16	14.40	11.44	11.44	11.44	11.44	11.44	8.00	8.00	8.00	8.00	8.00	8.00
Noncommercial rate	28.46	28.46	28.46	28.46	28.46	28.46	28.46	28.46	28.46	28.46	28.46	28.46	28.46	28.46	28.46	—	—	—	—	—	—	—	—	—
End period																								
(In leks per U.S. dollar)																								
Official rate	5.00	5.00	5.00	4.60	4.60	4.10	4.10	3.90	4.10	4.10	3.80	3.50	3.30	3.30	3.30	3.30	3.30	3.30	—	—	—	—	—	—
Commercial rate	14.4	14.4	14.4	13.25	13.25	11.80	11.80	11.23	11.80	11.80	10.95	10.10	9.50	8.58	8.58	8.58	8.58	8.58	8.00	8.00	8.00	8.00	10.00[2]	10.00
Noncommercial rate	10.00	10.00	10.00	10.00	9.20	8.20	8.20	7.80	8.20	8.20	7.60	7.00	7.00	7.00	7.00	7.00	7.00	7.00	—	—	—	—	—	—
(In leks per ruble)																								
Official rate	5.5555	5.5555	5.5555	5.5555	5.5555	5.5555	5.5555	5.5555	5.5555	5.5555	5.5555	5.5555	5.00	4.40	4.40	4.40	4.40	4.40	—	—	—	—	—	—
Commercial rate	16	16	16	16	16	16	15	16	16	16	16	16	14.40	11.44	11.44	11.44	11.44	11.44	8.00	8.00	8.00	8.00	8.00	8.00
Noncommercial rate	28.46	28.46	28.46	28.46	28.46	28.46	28.46	28.46	28.46	28.46	28.46	28.46	28.46	28.46	28.46	—	—	—	—	—	—	—	—	—

[1] Official exchange rates were used for accounting and statistical purposes up to 1985 and commercial exchange rates were used thereafter. Before 1986, the commercial exchange rates were not announced but were calculated and known as the economic exchange rates. The economic/commercial exchange rates were calculated by relating the total value of exports in U.S. dollars (rubles) valued at domestic wholesale prices to their values expressed in U.S. dollars (rubles).
[2] Rate changed to leks 10 on July 1.
[3] Buying rate from residents established on August 1.

Recent Occasional Papers of the International Monetary Fund

98. Albania: From Isolation Toward Reform, by Mario I. Blejer, Mauro Mecagni, Ratna Sahay, Richard Hides, Barry Johnston, Piroska Nagy, and Roy Pepper. 1992.

97. Rules and Discretion in International Economic Policy, by Manuel Guitián. 1992.

96. Policy Issues in the Evolving International Monetary System, by Morris Goldstein, Peter Isard, Paul R. Masson, and Mark P. Taylor. 1992.

95. The Fiscal Dimensions of Adjustment in Low-Income Countries, by Karim Nashashibi, Sanjeev Gupta, Claire Liuksila, Henri Lorie, and Walter Mahler. 1992.

94. Tax Harmonization in the European Community: Policy Issues and Analysis, edited by George Kopits. 1992.

93. Regional Trade Arrangements, by Augusto de la Torre and Margaret R. Kelly. 1992.

92. Stabilization and Structural Reform in the Czech and Slovak Federal Republic: First Stage, by Bijan B. Aghevli, Eduardo Borensztein, and Tessa van der Willigen. 1992.

91. Economic Policies for a New South Africa, edited by Desmond Lachman and Kenneth Bercuson with a staff team comprising Daudi Ballali, Robert Corker, Charalambos Christofides, and James Wein. 1992.

90. The Internationalization of Currencies: An Appraisal of the Japanese Yen, by George S. Tavlas and Yuzuru Ozeki. 1992.

89. The Romanian Economic Reform Program, by Dimitri G. Demekas and Mohsin S. Khan. 1991.

88. Value-Added Tax: Administrative and Policy Issues, edited by Alan A. Tait. 1991.

87. Financial Assistance from Arab Countries and Arab Regional Institutions, by Pierre van den Boogaerde. 1991.

86. Ghana: Adjustment and Growth, 1983–91, by Ishan Kapur, Michael T. Hadjimichael, Paul Hilbers, Jerald Schiff, and Philippe Szymczak. 1991.

85. Thailand: Adjusting to Success—Current Policy Issues, by David Robinson, Yangho Byeon, and Ranjit Teja with Wanda Tseng. 1991.

84. Financial Liberalization, Money Demand, and Monetary Policy in Asian Countries, by Wanda Tseng and Robert Corker. 1991.

83. Economic Reform in Hungary Since 1968, by Anthony R. Boote and Janos Somogyi. 1991.

82. Characteristics of a Successful Exchange Rate System, by Jacob A. Frenkel, Morris Goldstein, and Paul R. Masson. 1991.

81. Currency Convertibility and the Transformation of Centrally Planned Economies, by Joshua E. Greene and Peter Isard. 1991.

80. Domestic Public Debt of Externally Indebted Countries, by Pablo E. Guidotti and Manmohan S. Kumar. 1991.

79. The Mongolian People's Republic: Toward a Market Economy, by Elizabeth Milne, John Leimone, Franek Rozwadowski, and Padej Sukachevin. 1991.

78. Exchange Rate Policy in Developing Countries: Some Analytical Issues, by Bijan B. Aghevli, Mohsin S. Khan, and Peter J. Montiel. 1991.

77. Determinants and Systemic Consequences of International Capital Flows, by Morris Goldstein, Donald J. Mathieson, David Folkerts-Landau, Timothy Lane, J. Saúl Lizondo, and Liliana Rojas-Suárez. 1991.

76. China: Economic Reform and Macroeconomic Management, by Mario Blejer, David Burton, Steven Dunaway, and Gyorgy Szapary. 1991.

75. German Unification: Economic Issues, edited by Leslie Lipschitz and Donogh McDonald. 1990.

74. The Impact of the European Community's Internal Market on the EFTA, by Richard K. Abrams, Peter K. Cornelius, Per L. Hedfors, and Gunnar Tersman. 1990.

73. The European Monetary System: Developments and Perspectives, by Horst Ungerer, Jouko J. Hauvonen, Augusto Lopez-Claros, and Thomas Mayer. 1990.

72. The Czech and Slovak Federal Republic: An Economy in Transition, by Jim Prust and an IMF Staff Team. 1990.

71. MULTIMOD Mark II: A Revised and Extended Model, by Paul Masson, Steven Symansky, and Guy Meredith. 1990.

70. The Conduct of Monetary Policy in the Major Industrial Countries: Instruments and Operating Procedures, by Dallas S. Batten, Michael P. Blackwell, In-Su Kim, Simon E. Nocera, and Yuzuru Ozeki. 1990.

69. International Comparisons of Government Expenditure Revisited: The Developing Countries, 1975–86, by Peter S. Heller and Jack Diamond. 1990.

68. Debt Reduction and Economic Activity, by Michael P. Dooley, David Folkerts-Landau, Richard D. Haas, Steven A. Symansky, and Ralph W. Tryon. 1990.

67. The Role of National Saving in the World Economy: Recent Trends and Prospects, by Bijan B. Aghevli, James M. Boughton, Peter J. Montiel, Delano Villanueva, and Geoffrey Woglom. 1990.

66. The European Monetary System in the Context of the Integration of European Financial Markets, by David Folkerts-Landau and Donald J. Mathieson. 1989.

65. Managing Financial Risks in Indebted Developing Countries, by Donald J. Mathieson, David Folkerts-Landau, Timothy Lane, and Iqbal Zaidi. 1989.

64. The Federal Republic of Germany: Adjustment in a Surplus Country, by Leslie Lipschitz, Jeroen Kremers, Thomas Mayer, and Donogh McDonald. 1989.

63. Issues and Developments in International Trade Policy, by Margaret Kelly, Naheed Kirmani, Miranda Xafa, Clemens Boonekamp, and Peter Winglee. 1988.

62. The Common Agricultural Policy of the European Community: Principles and Consequences, by Julius Rosenblatt, Thomas Mayer, Kasper Bartholdy, Dimitrios Demekas, Sanjeev Gupta, and Leslie Lipschitz. 1988.

61. Policy Coordination in the European Monetary System. Part I: The European Monetary System: A Balance Between Rules and Discretion, by Manuel Guitián. Part II: Monetary Coordination Within the European Monetary System: Is There a Rule? by Massimo Russo and Giuseppe Tullio. 1988.

60. Policies for Developing Forward Foreign Exchange Markets, by Peter J. Quirk, Graham Hacche, Viktor Schoofs, and Lothar Weniger. 1988.

59. Measurement of Fiscal Impact: Methodological Issues, edited by Mario I. Blejer and Ke-Young Chu. 1988.

58. The Implications of Fund-Supported Adjustment Programs for Poverty: Experiences in Selected Countries, by Peter S. Heller, A. Lans Bovenberg, Thanos Catsambas, Ke-Young Chu, and Parthasarathi Shome. 1988.

57. The Search for Efficiency in the Adjustment Process: Spain in the 1980s, by Augusto Lopez-Claros. 1988.

56. Privatization and Public Enterprises, by Richard Hemming and Ali M. Mansoor. 1988.

55. Theoretical Aspects of the Design of Fund-Supported Adjustment Programs: A Study by the Research Department of the International Monetary Fund. 1987.

54. Protection and Liberalization: A Review of Analytical Issues, by W. Max Corden. 1987.

Note: For information on the title and availability of Occasional Papers not listed, please consult the IMF *Publications Catalog* or contact IMF Publication Services.